IS THAT LOVE OR WHAT?

GERDA'S STORY

To Stevie

[signature]

BOOKS BY LYLE E. HERBAUGH

You're Not Smart Enough to Do That
Stories from my life

Doubt and Redemption

Is That Love or What?
Gerda's Story

IS THAT LOVE OR WHAT?

GERDA'S STORY

BY

LYLE E. HERBAUGH

www.bookstandpublishing.com

Published by
Bookstand Publishing
Morgan Hill, CA 95037
4503_2

ISBN 978-1-63498-485-0

Printed in the United States of America

PREFACE

I LOVE YOU

I love your smile
I love your frown
I love your eyes
   When they sparkle
   And when they are sad.

I love your hair
   When it is combed
   And when it's not

I love your laughter
   And your tears

I love everything about you
I guess
I simply love you

—By Lyle E. Herbaugh

ACKNOWLEDGEMENTS

To my wife for her patience and support. Thank you to all of the nurses in the Skagit Regional Cancer Care Center for their support and encouragement. They all loved Gerda and wanted to know her story. During her illness, the nurses were wonderful, treating Gerda with love, tenderness and compassion. Never have we known more caring and compassionate professionals. Thank you very much.

ACKNOWLEDGMENTS

PROLOGUE

July 21, 2016 was my 80th birthday. If you look at the numbers for life expectancy of a male in the state of Washington, I should have died at 77.52 years. I have lived two years on borrowed time. When I wrote, "You're Not Smart Enough to Do That" I focused on my life and my achievements, both professional and private. I spent very little time telling about the family, especially my wife Gerda. Her early life was much more interesting than mine and her story deserves to be told. The developmental years of our three children were hectic and at times, difficult for them because of my moving from one job to the next. Several of those moves involved moving from Germany to the U.S. and then, two years later moving from the U.S. to Germany. We did that four times.

As our lives slow down we have more time to think about things, and like most older folks, we grow nostalgic and wonder if the "good old days" really were so good. If they were better than today, why were they better? We find life today to be very comfortable. Our house is warm in the winter and cool in the summer. We have 250 channels of television augmented by unlimited amounts of entertainment from Netflix, YouTube, Hulu, Crackle, and numerous other internet sites. Books are inexpensive via Amazon Kindle or Barnes and Noble Nook. The best music is available any time of the day or night, anywhere in the country, by streaming to a smart phone or pad. There is so much information available that it sometimes hurts my head. If I really want a headache from information overload, I can join Twitter, Instagram, Facebook, or any one of many social media sites. With all of this at our fingertips, if we get bored, it is our own fault. If we get confused, it's normal. But we still grow nostalgic and find ourselves looking backwards to a time that was our life, that is now only memories, some good, some very good, and a few bad ones.

I sometimes look forward and wonder how many more years I can get out of this old body. I also wonder what awaits me when the time comes to die. Will my belief in God assure me a place in Heaven or will some of my actions in my younger years outweigh the good deeds of my later life? Then there is the big question, does heaven exist at all, or will the lights go out and the curtain come down on this performance, and that is the end of the show? I will know soon enough, but I promise you that I will not tell you how it ends. It will remain my secret.

CONTENTS

INTRODUCTION

Our life together started in October 1959 when I arrived in Wiesbaden, Germany where I was serving in the U.S. Air Force. I suppose it actually started in 1945, at the end of the Second World War. My second cousin, Glen A. Davison, was part of the occupation forces following the surrender of Germany, ending the war in Europe. Glen had been part of the allied forces on "D" Day in June of 1944. He was a cartographer whom General Eisenhower had met over a year before in a walk-through inspection. Ike liked Glen's work so well that when the allies started planning the invasion, Ike asked for Glen to be brought up to his staff to draw the maps of the French coast. He, and several others, spent months building a detailed scale model of the coast, complete with cliffs, beaches, and bunkers. Using this model, the generals planned the invasion.

After the war, Glen asked to stay in Germany as part of the occupation forces. He was assigned to Headquarters U.S. Army Air Corp in Wiesbaden, Germany. He was the U.S. game warden for the Taunus Mountains and was responsible for issuing hunting licenses to the U.S. military personnel, and controlling the poaching done by hungry Germans. He worked directly under the Commander-in-Chief, General Curtis Lemay, and accompanied him on several hunting trips, including a lion-hunting trip to Africa.

Glen also managed a printing plant for the Army where he was in charge of writing and printing the wartime history of the third Armored Division. One of his office workers was a young German woman who was friends with my wife's sister, Irmgard. Irmgard would come by the printing plant on her lunch break, and there she met Glen. I won't say it was love at first sight, but they struck up a courtship which ended in 1948 when she flew to Washington D.C. and married Glen. She was a true war bride. When Glen separated from the Army, they moved to Sedro-Woolley. A year later, they moved to Mount Vernon, where they spent the next 50 years.

In 1956, Irmgard's mother, Elisabeth, came to Mount Vernon and spent the summer with Irmgard and Glen's family. During her stay, we had a large family reunion in Hillcrest Park in Mount Vernon, and she attended. I came home from Spokane, where I was stationed, to attend the reunion, where I was introduced to Elisabeth. She spoke no English, and I spoke no German, but we did exchange smiles and a lot of gestures. We seemed to communicate a little bit.

In the summer of 1959, I left the Island of Okinawa heading for my next assignment in Wiesbaden, Germany. While I was home on leave, I visited Irmgard and asked for her mother's address. I thought I would just drop in and say hello. At first she didn't want to give it to me, but she relented and gave me the address, and something else. She showed me a picture of Gerda, whom I didn't know existed. I was smitten. I looked at the picture, and I knew, without a doubt, that I was looking at my future wife. I don't know how, but I knew it.

It is now 56 years later and we are still together. During the years, Gerda has told me the stories of her youth and of the war. After several years of marriage, we found that we spent a lot of time talking. When potential conflict arose, we didn't fight, we talked and found a solution to the problem. We haven't spoken a cross word to each other in the last 25 years. I will attempt to tell her story just the way she described things to me. I make no attempt to tell what she was thinking and feeling, other than what she told me.

I write these stories for our grandchildren and their children, hoping that it will help them understand who their grandmother was and how she lived her life.

So, where do I start? I suppose the beginning would be a good place.

CHAPTER ONE

IN THE BEGINNING, THERE WAS WAR

Gerda's father, Ludwig Boucher, was born in Mainz, Germany on April 15, 1905. The family was not rich but had sufficient money to live a comfortable life. His parents owned and operated a *Gaststaette* or restaurant in Mainz. Some people would call it a *Kneipe*. They owned the building in which the *Kneipe* was located, and they lived in the apartment above it, thus they were able to enjoy all of the income it generated. A *Kneipe* is basically, what we in this country would call a tavern, in Britain it would be a pub. They served beer and wine, and had simple food items available such as pickled eggs, and B*ockwurst* (Frankfurter).

Unlike a tavern, the *Kneipe* was frequently the center of the community activities. Men gathered in the evenings to play cards. Every *Kneipe* had a *Stammtisch* where the men sat. It held an almost sacred status and no one sat at the *Stammtisch* except the men. The women also gathered and knitted, crocheted, and gossiped about whatever the theme was for the day. There was frequently singing and music. Germans love to sing and never missed a chance to break into song. Each community had a *Maennerchor* (men's choir) and the local chorus gathered once a week at the Boucher *Kneipe*. Children were allowed and Ludwig and his siblings often spent their evenings there, thus from an early age he was exposed to music and to the adult world.

Ludwig was full of life and loved a practical joke. He was a good storyteller and musician, and became a very accomplished accordion player. He played some piano, but he could make music with almost anything. A talent that would one day save his life. He was the class clown and enjoyed everything he did. As a young boy, he loved the silent movies. He and his friends would sit in the front row and at the exciting places in the film; they would shout their approval and throw their caps in the air. There was no sound track to interfere with so this kind of behavior was tolerated and maybe even enjoyed by the other guests. His future looked bright with exciting possibilities, but at the age of nine, war burst across Europe, changing everything.

****

Gerda's mother Elisabeth Zimmet was born in the small country town of *Katzenelnbogen* on April12, 1906. Literally translated the name of the town means "The Cat's Elbow", however the town has nothing to do with a cat's elbow. It is named after its founder, the Earl of *Katzenelnbogen*, who was a wealthy robber baron who had a castle on the Rhine River and forced anyone traveling the river to pay a tax. It was a good business because the Rhine River was the center of commerce in the 11th century.

Her father was a *Zimmerman* (Master carpenter) and as such was highly respected in the town. He was especially skilled in building the half-timber houses of the time. They were not wealthy but made ends meet by supplementing their diet with homegrown vegetables from their own garden. Her mother was a homemaker and garden work was considered women's work, so she was responsible for their garden and livestock. Elisabeth loved to work in the garden and learned at a very young age the benefits of hard work and the pleasure of enjoying the fruits of her labor.

In the center of the town was *Schloss Katzenelnbogen* sitting high on a hill overlooking the town.

Like most small towns of that time, there was no work for the young people especially the women. Most of them migrated to the bigger cities and found work as domestic servants working as maids, cooks, and wait staff. Elisabeth moved to Wiesbaden and found work in a fairly wealthy household. She would do so when she was only 16, but first, when she was eight, war came to Europe.

CHAPTER TWO

WORLD WAR I

T he First World War seemed to start by accident. In 1914, Germany was the second largest economy in the world, falling just behind the United States of America. With economic dominance in Europe, war was not on the minds of the German people. They had a large standing army and believed that no country was a threat to their economic and military dominance. The U.S. was far away and not at all interested in what was happening in Europe. The future was bright for both Ludwig and Elisabeth.

The war raged for four years; however, Germany was never invaded by foreign soldiers. The allies of France, England, The Netherlands, and Belgium fought the entire war in the trenches of France and the Low Countries. In the East, Germany defeated Russia in spite of the fact that Russia had the largest standing army in the world in 1914. They had more troops than they had guns with which to equip them. To make matters worse, they were poorly trained. Many of them trained with fake wooden guns.

The British Navy established a blockade around Germany making it impossible for them to continue with trading and exporting their products. Imports were also limited and it wasn't long until food items became scarce and everyone was required to limit their consumption. Much of the food was needed to feed the army and was directed to the military. Many items were rationed and the economy slowed to a crawl. By 1918, even though Germany was never invaded, the war was not going well on either front and the economy had collapsed. The allies met in Versailles' and drew up the terms of surrender which they presented to Germany along with the ultimatum "take it or be destroyed." Germany took it. On November 11, 1918, they surrendered and the war was over. By that time, Germany was no longer the second strongest economy and much of the population was hungry or starving.

CHAPTER THREE

MASS STARVATION AND THE GOLDEN YEARS

The Treaty of Versailles dictated that Germany pay billions of dollars in reparations, far beyond what was realistic for them to repay. The allies also continued their blockade and trade was severely limited. The food shortage became critical and many civilians died of starvation. The exact number is not known. It was rumored in the west that millions survived by eating sauerkraut. Cabbage was easy to grow and the sauerkraut would keep for months without spoiling. Because of that rumor, the Germans became known in slang as "Krauts". The blockade was lifted in July of 1919.

In 1921, Germany could not pay and French and Belgium troops invaded and occupied the Ruhr Valley, and took the goods and raw materials. The downhill skid continued and in 1923, Germany started printing more and more money to pay the workers. Hyperinflation resulted and the value of the currency collapsed. Everyone felt the pain.

The years 1924 to 1929 were known as the golden years. Germany became increasingly prosperous and peaceful. The USA had loaned Germany huge sums of money. The economy was rebuilt, unemployment was reduced, and people, once again, began to feel secure.

Things were looking good for both Elisabeth and Ludwig. He completed an apprenticeship and was a fully trained baker. To find work he moved across the Rhine River to Wiesbaden. Elisabeth also moved to Wiesbaden and worked in a wealthy household where she did housekeeping and completed an apprenticeship in food preparation. She became an accomplished cook.

The circumstances surrounding their meeting are not known, however, in late 1926 they were married in the *Ringkirche* in Wiesbaden. They first moved to *Katzenelnbogen* where on May 16, 1927, their first daughter, Irmgard, was born. Life was good, and the future was bright.

Ludwig, Elisabeth and Irmgard.

Lyle E. Herbaugh

CHAPTER FOUR

FROM BOOM TO BUST

October 1929, the stock market in New York crashed causing a run on the banks. The Great Depression started. Because of the extensive business ties between the U.S. and Europe, the falling U.S. economy dragged the rest of the world into the depression. The U.S. had loaned Germany vast amounts of money and the banks wanted their money back. Germany could not pay and defaulted.

Unemployment rose rapidly and by 1932 Germany was suffering with 30 percent of the country unemployed. The bright future suddenly disappeared leaving only hopelessness in its place. Elisabeth was able to continue working, but Ludwig struggled. He worked at anything he could find. He picked up garbage, swept the streets, baked, and did his best. Finally, an opening occurred in the Wiesbaden Post Office. Overnight he became a letter carrier. This was remarkable since almost twenty million people were looking for work. Many were homeless and lived in city parks in Berlin.

Ludwig was a serious and loyal worker, and soon gained a reputation for reliability and credibility. The post office provided only a modest income, but it kept the family fed and a roof over their heads. Because of bank failures, almost everyone lost any savings they might have had. Then in 1933, the NAZI party came to power. Everything changed.

Shortly after taking power in 1933, Hitler began the purification of society. Every city in Germany was divided into sectors. Sizes varied from city to city but the object always remained the same; to control the people living in that sector. Attending community meetings became a must; work parties were formed to beautify the city and participation was mandatory.

To maintain control, each block had a NAZI controller and each building had one. The building controller would make a point of reminding folks of a meeting or work party, and then record the attendance to ensure that everyone did their duty. If you missed a meeting you were soon visited by one of the controllers, who made it very clear that you must attend, or you would be dealt with accordingly.

Ludwig hated the requirements and restrictions and sometimes refused to attend the meetings. On a visit from the building controller he was warned that if he missed another meeting the controller must report the absence to his superior. Ludwig responded with "your superior can kiss my ass." Ludwig was immediately reminded by the controller that if he reported that statement to his superior, Ludwig would be arrested and interned in a labor camp. He chose not to report the incident and Ludwig was not arrested. He decided to keep his thoughts to himself and managed to stay out of trouble.

The main focus of the NAZI party was the training and indoctrination of the youth. Organizations were established for both boys and girls. Boys age 6 to 10 belonged to the *Jungvolk* and from 14 to 18 were in the *Hitler Jugend* (Hitler Youth). Young boys from 6 to 10 were allowed to hang around the older boys and sometimes participate informally in the activities. Devotion to Hitler was an important and central component of Hitler Youth training.

Girls 10 to 14 joined the *Jungmaedel* and those 14 to 18 belonged to the *Bund Deutscher Maedel* (League of German Girls). They wore uniforms with skirts and blouses and army-style boots. Both of Gerda's older sisters participated with relative enthusiasm. They loved the activities and comradery and enjoyed the meetings a great deal.

The indoctrination began early in life. From the first day in school the children were introduced to Hitler. His picture hung in every classroom. The textbooks were altered to teach students love for Hitler, obedience to state authority, militarism, racism and antisemitism. Board games and toys were also used as tools to indoctrinate children into militarism.

The objective of the youth organizations and schools was designed to produce race-conscious, obedient, self-sacrificing Germans, willing to die for their Fuehrer and country. To create a nation where everyone knew their place and fulfilled their duty. Where everyone was honest and trustworthy, a place where crime was rare but if it occurred it was punished swiftly and justly.

When Gerda entered the first grade she was taught how to salute properly with her right arm extended with the palm down. Every morning they started the day with a salute and a pledge of allegiance to Hitler and pledged to serve the nation and its leader.

Lyle E. Herbaugh

CHAPTER FIVE

WAR AGAIN

Unlike World War I, at the end of World War II German cities were in complete ruin. Every major city was destroyed. Railroads and train stations were useless. The highway system was damaged, but large areas remained intact. Services like gas, water and electricity were, for the most part, non-existent.

The British, in response to Hitler's bombing of London during the Battle of Britain, blanket bombed the cities, regardless of their military significance. They bombed during the night when it was more difficult for the ground anti-aircraft gun crews to see them. The U.S. preferred daylight precision bombing from very high altitudes. Either way, the object was to destroy the people's will to support the war. It was a terrible inhumane approach to winning a war.

The Second WW and its impact on Germany is beyond imagination. It touched every man, woman and child in the country, and in every European and African country invaded and occupied by Germany. When the allies liberated France, Belgium, and the Netherlands, in order to dislodge the German soldiers, it was necessary to destroy entire towns. The same thing held true for the Eastern front. The damage to all of Europe was extensive.

The city of Cologne, Germany.

Berlin, Germany, at the end of the war.

Now back to the war. It wasn't long after Germany invaded Poland that Ludwig was drafted into the army. Because he was trained in the postal service he was assigned to the *Feldpost* or field post office. His unit was usually a few miles behind the fighting units, and it was their job to get the mail to the men on the front lines. If a breakthrough happened the fighting could and did rapidly involve the *Feldpost*. That is what happened following the siege of Stalingrad.

Ludwig was assigned to the Russian front supporting a *Schutzstaffel* or SS unit. He was never required to join the SS because he was not assigned to a direct unit, but only in a support role. They had been involved in a battle and were in full retreat mode. At one point, they became surrounded on three sides by the Russian Army and on the forth side by a river running full of ice. A few weeks earlier it would have been frozen solid and would not have presented a problem. Now it was during the spring thaw and was full of ice chunks. The choice was to attempt to swim the river or be killed by the Russians.

Since his unit was supporting a SS unit Ludwig knew that the Russians would not ask questions but would summarily execute them. He chose the river. By this time Ludwig was in his late thirties while most of the other men in his unit and the SS unit were many years younger. Hundreds went into the river but only a few climbed out on the other side. Ludwig survived when so many of the younger men did not. They did not have the tenacity and the will to live that he had, and that made the difference.

It made little difference because he was captured and moved to a prisoner of war camp where he stayed for several months. Exactly where the camp was located and how long he was imprisoned, we don't know, but before the end of the war he escaped and fled to Berlin. How did he escape when the POW camp was in the middle of nowhere?

Ludwig was very musical with many talents; one was the ability to make music anywhere on almost anything. He was assigned to kitchen duty in the officer's club one evening when he noticed that the pots and pans were hung on pegs on the wall with their bottoms facing outwards. He got an idea. He hung them according to their size and taking two wooden cook spoons, he began to beat a rhythm on the pots. This immediately got the attention of the officers who started to sing along with the beat. Most of them had already consumed a good supply of vodka which tempered their judgement.

They asked Ludwig what else he played and when he told them, soon an accordion appeared. From that day on, he was known as "Ludwig the musician". He was taken off of the other duty assignments and became the official entertainment for the officers. Soon he was given a great amount of freedom to wander and come and go as he wanted, and one evening, when the show was over and the officers were full of vodka he wandered out of the gate and headed west. He made it to Berlin. He never told us how he made it to Berlin, nor did he explain many details of his life in the POW camp. Following the surrender of Germany, Ludwig made his way to Wiesbaden and home. The war for everyone in the family was over. Now they had to find a way to survive the years to come. Ludwig found a way.

CHAPTER SIX

THE WAR COMES HOME

From ages two to eight Gerda spent the nights in bomb shelters or cellars, listening to bombs fall, feeling the ground rise and fall and the buildings shake as the bombs exploded. The noise was deafening. At first, the family went into the cellar of the building where they lived. All of the families in the building would rush to the basement as soon as the sirens began to wail. Then they would return to the apartments when the all clear sounded. This could happen several times during the night, so they moved some things into the cellar for the children to sleep on and everyone moved to the cellar and stayed for the entire night. How the adults slept, I am not sure? In the house where Gerda lived they built some bunk beds out of wood and the children were laid there to sleep. Much of the time the adults shared the bunks with the children.

Every family member had a gasmask, even the children. When it was time to go to the cellar, Gerda would grab her little gasmask and hurry down the steps to the protection of the basement. Since the allies didn't use chemical weapons, she never had to use her mask. They did, however, practice how to take it out of its bag and put it on as fast as possible. All of these things made a lasting impression on the children. When the adults showed fear, and cried, it upset the children. They were too young to know what it all meant, but when the parents were afraid, they were afraid. When the mothers cried, the children cried. When the bombing was at its worst the adults would huddle together and hold their children close to them. The buildings shook and the sound of the explosions was deafening, and everyone was terrified waiting for the next one to hit their house and end it all. Gerda didn't understand what was happening, but she knew she hated the loud noise and the feeling of fear that filled the cellar.

To provide for an escape route in case of fire, the men opened a hole in the cellar wall so everyone could move from house to house. In Gerda's neighborhood, you could go the entire city block underground. For security, the openings were filled with loose bricks which could be rapidly removed if necessary.

In each cellar, there was a pile of sand for use in extinguishing fires caused by incendiary bombs. The children were trained to use the sand. In case of a fire they were to pour sand on it. Gerda never had to do that, so the sand pile became a place for the children to play. They had few toys, so they used small pieces of wood or stones for toys. On some nights when they turned over a rock or brick, they found little gray insects called *Kellerassel*, which they played with. Bug races were fun and exciting.

The city of Wiesbaden was only ten percent destroyed, while Mainz, just across the Rhine River was over 90 percent destroyed. The story that was told to the American pilots was that a plane had been shot down over Mainz and the crew parachuted to a safe landing. They were immediately attacked by the German civilians and beaten to death. The standing order to the aircrews was that if their primary target was weathered in, they should target Mainz and drop their load of bombs there. Mainz was also a major railroad hub where vast amounts of freight moved every day. This made it a primary target for many of the bombing raids.

One night during a bombing raid, a building housing a bakery was hit with a large bomb. The bakery kept huge amounts of flour in the neighboring basement. The explosion blew out the wall and flour filled the air suffocating everyone in the cellar. Word spread quickly, and everyone started moving to a public shelter several blocks from where Gerda and her family lived. When the air-raid sirens sounded, they would grab their coats, and gasmasks and run to the shelter. After the raid, the all clear would sound and they would return to their homes.

The area of Wiesbaden that was destroyed was only a few blocks from where the family lived, and near to the public shelter, so the explosions were loud and the ground moved like an earthquake. Mainz was close enough that the bombing there could be heard in Wiesbaden, and no one knew exactly what was going to happen next. When the sirens wailed, no one knew which city would be bombed. Adults and children alike were in fear that the next bomb could be a direct hit on the shelter.

After leaving the shelter following a bombing raid on Wiesbaden, the family was hurrying home to their apartment when a house exploded. They were across the street from a four-story apartment house when suddenly the entire house seemed to rise and then collapse. A giant ball of fire rose hundreds of feet into the air. A delayed action incendiary bomb had hit the house and penetrated all the way to the cellar where it lay until Gerda and her family were right next to it. Because the bomb was in the cellar, the blast wave was directed upwards and passed over their heads. Everyone was terrified, and Gerda cried for the rest of the night. That explosion was so real that she had frequent nightmares about it for many years. We had been married for 20 years when she had her last nightmare. To this day, she still talks about that house and gets upset.

Both during the war and after it ended, materials to repair broken windows or other damaged things were not available. During the war, everything was needed to support the military and the war. Afterwards it was needed to rebuild the country. Folks just made do with whatever they had or could find.

The house where Gerda was living had a broken window in the stairway leading to the cellar. One day she was hurrying to the cellar when a neighbor boy who was mentally challenged, pushed her and she fell against the broken window. A piece of glass that was still lodged in the frame cut her arm between her wrist and elbow. It was a deep cut several inches long. She needed stiches to close the cut, but there was no doctor available to treat the cut, and the family had no way of stitching it themselves. They bound her arm with a clean towel and applied pressure until the bleeding stopped. It healed, but it left a large scar on her left arm.

The war dragged on, and the bombing continued. Food and other supplies became more and more scarce. With Ludwig away Elisabeth had to make all the decisions. She remembered the gardens of her youth and of the peace and quiet of *Katzenelnbogen*. She decided it was time to go home and ride out the rest of the war where the family would be reasonably safe.

**The house in KatzeneInbogen with two aunts
and two cousins.**

They had a small four wheeled wagon they could pull by hand, so they loaded a few things in the wagon and headed for *Katzenelnbogen*. Elisabeth, Irmgard, Gisela, and Gerda walked the thirty miles pulling the wagon. They made it safely and moved in with Elisabeth's father, sister and family.

Life immediately changed for the family. The town had a public bunker, but they seldom needed to go there. The town was never bombed because it was small and had no military significance. The planes flew over the town by the hundreds. The Americans were daylight bombing the cities and factories of Germany and flew directly over the little town. Sometimes it would take an hour for all of the bombers to fly past, always on their way to somewhere else.

Right behind the house were some stone cliffs that to Gerda seemed like giant mountains of stone. She would climb on the stones, playing make believe games that she created in her childish fantasy. It was as if she had died and gone to heaven. No bombs falling, no houses exploding, and no noises of war.

The war seemed like it was in another world and then the Canadian military arrived. They were the first to reach the town of *Katzenelnbogen*, followed a few hours later by the Americans. Even though a group of old men were protecting the town, they wisely decided not to defend it against the overwhelming power of the Canadians and Americans.

No shots were fired, and the town quietly surrendered. During the approach of the Allies they fired several artillery shells into the town, one of which damaged the roof of the family home. During this shelling most of the town residents took shelter in the town bunker. An American tank rolled up in front of the bunker and gave the command to surrender or they would destroy the bunker and everyone inside. The old men were afraid to go out, so Irmgard tied a white cloth to a broom handle and surrendered the bunker.

The Three Sisters, Irmgard, Gisela and Gerda.

The American Army needed quarters for their officers and someplace to set up a command post. They moved several families out of their homes and took control of them. They liked the family house because it was situated on a hill

25

overlooking the town, which would give the Army oversight of the town in case of any counterattack. They received word to evacuate the house. The women were crying and the men were trying to decide where they could go, and how they could survive.

Irmgard, who was 18, went to see the commander and explained that her grandfather was very ill and it would be extremely difficult to care for him if they had to move. She may have told him some other sad tales of woe but the commander relented and revoked the eviction notice, and the family could stay in their home.

It was pretty common for the American GIs to save their chocolate candy and give it to the German children. Someone gave Gerda a chocolate bar which she took home and asked what it was. She had never eaten chocolate in her life and didn't have any idea what it was. The grandfather immediately took it away from her and told her it was poison that the Americans were using, and that she should never take any and never eat any.

Before the Americans had arrived the older folks in the town had told the children that they were in grave danger because the invading army lived off the land and that they ate children. They were evil people who should be avoided at all cost.

CHAPTER SEVEN

THE POST-WAR RECOVERY

Within a few weeks, the war ended and it was time to return to Wiesbaden and see if their house was still standing. They loaded their things in the little wagon and headed home and to an unknown future.

What they found was destroyed houses, empty stores, nothing to buy and nothing to eat. Their house was intact and everything they had left behind was still right where they had left it. With the destruction of the cities and factories the economy died. There was nothing to buy so all the old stores were empty. The farmers had food and the city folks had some stuff, so in order to survive the barter system developed. If you had something a farmer could use, you traded it for food. Soon within the system a thriving black market emerged.

The old money was useless. The U.S. troops used a paper currency called "Script". From May 1945 until June 1948 there was no money for the entire German population. One thing emerged as good as gold. The American cigarette. It was in high demand. If you knew an American who was willing to sell you a carton of cigarettes and you had something he could use, you made a deal and suddenly you could buy food, clothes and almost anything that was available in the black market, with a cigarette. This demand would play a very important part of their lives in the weeks to come.

Any form of tobacco was valuable, even half smoked butts. The kids would walk the streets looking for any cigarette butts someone had discarded. The tobacco was then recycled into new cigarettes. They must have tasted terrible, but most people didn't smoke them, they used it as money. One day Gerda was out looking and saw an American soldier chewing on a big cigar. That would be a prize to behold, so she followed him until he threw it away. It was a big saliva filled cigar butt, but it could be dried and used again. She was thrilled.

When Gerda was born the attending nurse put silver nitrate in her eyes. This was the accepted practice to keep Gonorrhea from causing blindness in the children. It also prevented pink eye in newborns. Instead of the two percent solution, she used a stronger one which damaged Gerda' right eye. The muscles which control the lateral movement of the eye were damaged causing her right eye to turn inwards toward her nose. To correct this flaw, she had two surgeries, one during the war and a second one after the war. She remembers that the first surgery was done in the basement of the clinic, in case they were bombed during the procedure. The second in an eye clinic. The second surgery corrected the movement of the eye, but left her legally blind in that eye.

During this time of near famine, Gerda became very ill. She cried and complained of pains in the legs and joints. It was Rheumatic Fever. She also contracted a lung ailment, which had the symptoms of Tuberculosis, even though it was not diagnosed as such. If it had not been for the generous help of a neighbor and Irmgard's friend Glen, the ending could have been much different.

At the end of the war General George Marshall knew that without help thousands or even millions of Germans would starve to death. He developed and pushed through congress a plan to feed the starving nations of Europe. The Marshall Plan came to be. It provided food of all types for distribution in Germany and other war torn countries.

In spite of the Marshall Plan food was scarce, and when it was available, it was rationed. If there was butter, each family was allocated a few ounces. If meat was available, each family received a small amount for each person. The American military provided food for the school children. Gerda had a little metal plate and cup that she carried to school. There she was introduced to oatmeal mush, orange and grapefruit juice, and other typical American foods. The oatmeal was sometimes seasoned with chocolate, and sometimes with fruit flavors like blueberries. She ate everything they gave her. She fell in love with grapefruit juice. Through the years she drank liberal amounts of grapefruit juice.

During the time when she was sick, she was confined to bed for many weeks. When food was available she was given an extra ration. Her neighbor worked for the Americans and was served lunch at work. He always kept a little bit for Gerda even though he had his own children to feed. Glen had access to the American commissary and frequently brought food items to the family.

It was through Glen that Gerda ate her first banana. She started to eat the peel because she had never seen one, and didn't know that you had to remove the peel to get at the edible part. After a good laugh, Glen showed her how to do it.

During the Third Reich, it was the policy of the NAZI party that if it was not German, it was not available. Gerda had never seen an orange, grapefruit, a banana, or a pineapple, so this was all new and exciting for her.

Glen hunted as part of his duties, and when possible brought wild game, such as venison, wild boar or some type of game bird.

On one occasion, he brought a container of ice cream. There was little fuel with which to heat the apartment, so everyone sat in the cold and ate ice cream.

One day they were able to buy a ring of bologna and Gerda received an extra portion. The ring was divided among the family members. When Gerda finished her portion, she looked at the ring and wanted to know where her piece was.

The farmers were able to raise food and sold much of if through the black market. Many people did not have money or cigarettes with which to pay, so they did whatever it took to feed their families. Many made night raids to the farmers' fields and stole potatoes etc... Gerda' family made the trip to *Katzenelnbogen* to get potatoes or whatever was in season. There was a small gauge railroad that connected *Katzenelnbogen* to a small town near Wiesbaden. Sometimes the authorities would board the train and search for food items that might have been stolen. Whenever the train was boarded Gerda would lie down on the potato bag and go to sleep or fake it like she was sleeping. The inspectors never woke her up so the guise worked well.

****

Then Ludwig returned from the war. While living in Berlin, Ludwig had met someone and intended to stay in Berlin and restart his life after the turmoil of war. Elisabeth sent him pictures of the family and the apartment and he changed his mind and came home to the family. When he got home many things changed, and Gerda didn't like many of the changes.

Because of her illness and the horrors of war that Gerda was forced to live, her mother became a very liberal disciplinarian, and allowed Gerda considerable room to become a spoiled brat. In the evenings, the young adults gathered in an apartment in the same building and talked, listened to the radio, and drank a little beer. Gerda was allowed to go with her older sister and heard things that were not fit for her young ears, but she thought it was great. The first evening after Ludwig returned, she got ready to go down to the evening gathering. Her father asked her where she was going and when she told him, he immediately said "No you're not, it is past your bed time and you are going to bed". She told him that she was too going down stairs and he promptly boxed her ears and into bed she went.

A few days later Ludwig was playing keep away with her teddy bear, and at one point he threw it across the room. Gerda shouted at him and told him that she wished he had stayed in Russia. He responded by slapping her soundly on the cheek. Ludwig had been gone so long and Gerda was young enough that she had forgotten that this man was her father and was in charge whether she liked it or not. She now realized that she had better listen or she was going to get slapped around.

Ludwig returned to work at the post office and found that several of his co-workers were farmers who grew tobacco but didn't know how to cure it and process it into cigarettes. Ludwig was pretty sure he could do it, so he reached an agreement with them that he would take care of the task of turning raw tobacco into cigarettes. In turn he could keep a percentage of the cigarettes for his own use. He turned the entire apartment into a cigarette manufacturing plant.

He dried tobacco in the oven. He hung it on lines in the kitchen and living room. Before he could cure it, he had to wash it in a Potassium Nitrate (saltpeter) solution, then he could hang it out to dry. The entire apartment smelled of tobacco and saltpeter. When it was sufficiently dry, he rolled the leaves into tight tubes and cut it into shreds. To keep the leaves from crumbling he had to wet them just prior to rolling. Elisabeth had the task of rolling the leaves into a cigar shaped roll which had to be just the right size to fit in the shredder. Then it became a family affair to roll the cigarettes. Ludwig found a little cigarette roller and they started turning out the finished product. Suddenly they had something with which to buy food and other things on the black market.

Ludwig was not a very patient man so when anything went wrong he would fly off the handle. Elisabeth caught the brunt of his temper tantrums. He never struck her but there were always loud voices and shouting which made a lasting impression on Gerda. One which has lasted her entire life.

Everything smelled like tobacco and saltpeter, even their clothes and hair. Everyone hated the smell, but through tobacco Ludwig fed, housed, and clothed the family. In payment for the cigarettes the farmers provided eggs, potatoes and vegetables that were in season.

In addition to the tobacco he got from the farmers, Ludwig grew plants in flower pots on the window sills. Any cigarettes he could produce from these plants was all theirs which made them extra valuable.

****

As could be expected, there was a critical housing shortage. Immediately after the war ended the women and able bodied men took to the streets and reclaimed the building materials. Using a hammer if they had one, or using another brick they chipped the old mortar from the stones and bricks and piled them in preparation for rebuilding. Everyone who could work, did. Since Wiesbaden was only ten percent destroyed, the task was manageable. In cities like Mainz and Cologne or Berlin, it was a monumental task.

The provisional government was established to manage the affairs of state and the American Military oversaw their actions. One of their first priorities was to find a way of housing the millions of homeless. If you owned an apartment or house, you were told how many people could live in a given square meter of space and if your family didn't completely fill the space you had to take in renters. The family was told that they had excess space in their apartment and that they must take in some strangers. Ludwig did not want to do that, so he found a smaller place and they moved into an apartment that could accommodate their family with no space left over for strangers. They moved from *Sedanstrasse* to the West End of Wiesbaden to a little street that was only one block long, called *Lothringerstrasse*. That is where they lived the rest of their lives.

Following the return of the family from *Katzenelnbogen* and Ludwig from Berlin, their family filled the apartment and they were not affected by the rules to take in someone. During the period from 1945 to June 1948 they lived from the sale of tobacco and the black market. It was during this period that Gerda was ill and her sister Irmgard met Glen A. Davison.

Glen was managing an Army print shop and was writing and publishing the History of the 3rd Armored Division. It also printed a daily copy of the Stars and Stripes. A young German woman worked for him and she just happened to be Irmgard's best friend.

Irmgard frequently went to the print shop on her lunch break and as time went on they began to date. I use that term loosely, but they began to see each other outside of the print shop. Since the family had very little, and Glen had access to food and many other things, he helped them out when and where possible. Other soldiers were getting rich from the black market, but Glen never made a dime from the plight of the German civilians. Beside it being illegal, Glen considered it to be immoral to take advantage of someone else's misfortune.

One of the things that Glen was able to get on rare occasions was women's nylon stockings. They were a luxury item for any German woman to have. The first pair Irmgard got soon fell victim to Gerda. She was fascinated by the nylons and decided to try them on. Nylons were very fragile and would run (a hole would open and run the length of the stocking.) if stressed. In trying to put them on, Gerda literally destroyed them.

Another thing that met its match with Gerda was a bottle of French perfume that Glen gave to Irmgard. Gerda decided that she liked the scent very much and poured the entire bottle on her head and on her clothes. She smelled for days.

Glen was the game warden for the *Taunus* Mountain region of Germany and had access to all sorts of wild game. One day he came to the apartment with a little wild piglet that immediately became a smash hit with Gerda. Glen kept the piglet in his quarters for some time, but soon had to find a place for it. The piglet along with some other animals that Glen caught, became the Wiesbaden Animal Park.

In early 1948 Glen was reassigned to the Washington D.C. area, where he immediately started the paperwork to bring Irmgard to the United States. They had agreed that she would join him in Washington and they would be married. And so it was. In December 1948 Irmgard departed for Washington D.C. where they were married

When Irmgard left for the states it left some space in the apartment and they were notified that they must take in someone. That is when Ludwig moved the family to the new address. The move was not necessary but Ludwig had his mind made up and nothing would change it. Gerda' older sister Gisela became pregnant and moved with her husband into a tiny one room apartment which they shared with her mother-in-law. There was sufficient room in the *Sedanstrasse* apartment for them all, plus a small room for the baby, but Ludwig said no. "She made her bed, now she can lie in it." I don't think Gisela ever forgave him for that.

During the years that followed, Glen and Irmgard sent many care packages to the family. A big hit was the big three pound cans of MJB coffee. Coffee is loved by the Germans and it was very scarce at this time, so they were thrilled whenever a package arrived. Gerda received a lot of clothes, some of which were the latest fashions.

Many of the clothing items were the latest U.S. fashions, but not in Germany, so in typical young girl fashion, Gerda did not want to wear them. Other dresses and blouses were a great hit with her and her friends. One thing in particular was a Teddy Coat, which was quite expensive. At first she didn't want to wear it, but finally did and everyone wanted a coat just like it. Of course, Gerda loved the attention and wore the coat as often as she could.

Gerda's sister Gisela was a skilled seamstress and when cloth remnants were left over from customer ordered clothes, she made clothes for Gerda. Between Irmgard's care packages and Gisela's skilled hands, Gerda was well dressed in spite of the family having very limited funds.

CHAPTER EIGHT

COMING OF AGE

On 20 June 1948, the Deutsch Mark was created. Every man woman and child was given DM 40.00 followed a couple of weeks later with an additional DM 20.00. Suddenly you could buy anything and everything. Overnight the stores were filled with things to buy, clothing, food, hardware, anything. Germany was on its way to prosperity, and life was once again becoming normal and the future looked bright.

Gerda was ten that year, and was in school full time. She was very shy but full of devilment and had a very vivid imagination. She could think of ways to irritate the teachers, and convince someone else to perform the act. She was a master at stirring the pot.

One day the teacher left the room, and she immediately had a great idea. She and a friend climbed on top of a cabinet used to store supplies. It was dusty and uncomfortable but they stayed there until the teacher returned. They expected some sort of outburst, but nothing happened. The teacher obviously knew they were on top of the cabinet but he paid no attention to them. He merely left them there for the entire class.

Outside of school, her life was relatively normal. In the afternoon and early evening, she played with the neighborhood kids on the street. Some of the games were real games, but many of them they made up as they went along. One game was called "*Stadt-Land*". It was a game of world geography, and Gerda was always good and usually won. At that time of her life it was great fun, and she made many long-lasting friendships.

One of the neighborhood kids had a bicycle and tried to teach her how to ride. She soon got the feel and could balance it somewhat. At that time, almost no one had a car, so the streets were completely empty. On this particular day, there was one car parked at the end of the street. Gerda rode down the hill and right into the side of the car. She has never ridden a bicycle since.

One of the neighbors had an older car and took Gerda for a ride. What a thrill. This was the only car on the block and the woman was the only person Gerda knew who could drive. She climbed bravely into the front seat, and off they went. At the end of the block they slowly turned left. The door popped open and Gerda fell out of the car landing face down in the street. Her thrilling ride ended about where it had started. To this day, Gerda does not drive.

Every year at *Fastnacht* or Mardi Gras, the city of Wiesbaden held a parade on Sunday before Rose Monday. Many of the floats in the parade had people throwing candy into the crowd. Gerda refused to pick up any candy much to her father's dismay. To this day she doesn't know why she would not pick up candy from the street.

One of the jobs she disliked with a passion was picking up beechnuts. When times were hard and food was scarce, the family would go into the woods and find a beechnut tree and look for nuts. It was done in the fall when the nuts were ripe. They crawled around in the leaves looking for the nuts. A nut was about the size of a woman's little finger nail, and three sided. The nuts were then taken to the person who had an oil press and pressed producing cooking oil. The person kept some of the oil for the price of doing the work.

There were numerous other childish pranks she pulled, but let's move on to her apprenticeship in the lawyer's office.

****

It was common practice that at the age of 14 young people, both boys and girls, entered an apprenticeship. The parent decided what the child would learn and then found a business that would take their child and teach them a skill. The commitment was normally three years. During that time the student would spend three days in On-The-Job training, and 2 days in classroom training each week. The monthly pay was *30DM* per month during the first year, then *50DM* the second, and *70Dm* the third. It was a fantastic way to learn, and was the main reason that Germany had so many highly skilled craftsmen.

Ludwig decided that Gerda should become a legal secretary, and found her an apprenticeship in the law office of Dr. Hill whose office was in downtown Wiesbaden.

This time was known as *Lehrzeit* or learning time, and always started with the trainee being assigned simple tasks, and menial jobs. The office was heated with a single coal fired stove and one of Gerda' first jobs was to light the stove so the office would be warm when Doctor Hill arrived. The first time she did it, she overloaded the stove with coal and the heat became almost unbearable. The stove over heated and it could have been a disaster, but luck intervened and everything turned out ok.

One of her first office tasks was to learn bookkeeping. She was given a group of stamps of varying values and it was her responsibility to keep accountability, place postage on all of the outgoing mail, and reorder stamps when the supply grew low. She was then given money with which to buy the stamps. She made the trek to the post office, bought what was needed and returned. She had to balance the books, keeping track of the stamps and the money.

It sounds simple, but there was an enormous amount of lessons to be learned. Until now Gerda had never had any money. First there was none to be had because of the war, and the aftermath. Since she never received an allowance, this was all new and foreign territory for her. Now for the first time in her life she had some money to manage, some at work and some of her own. It wasn't much, but it was hers. She did, however, give some of her income to her mother to help cover the cost of food and lodging.

Over the next three years she became a skilled legal assistant. She found that she loved the rhythm and texture of the language of law. She devoured the text books and became the office walking law book. She passed her final exam and was ready for the big world. She was immediately hired by the municipal court of Wiesbaden as a court recorder. She was on her way.

Gerda learned shorthand and was quite proficient, but a court recorder could not take testimony in shorthand. She sat next to the judge and typed everything into a typewriter. That way if the witness needed to see a verbatim transcript she could remove the paper from the typewriter and the person could read what was said.

Later in the trial the judge would give her his comments and decision. He often quoted paragraph numbers from the law books, and she had to review the paragraph and include the wording in the decision. The judge would then sign the document she had prepared and it was on to the next case.

This system required very fast typing skills, and an understanding of the German language and of the contents of several law books. In law, the use of punctuation was very important because a comma could change the meaning of the entire sentence, and thus affect the outcome of the trial.

Gerda was good, and frequently finished her workload before some of the older and more experienced recorders did. She then helped them with their workload.

Gerda was a very pretty young lady and of course, caught the eye of lawyers and other court officials. Fraulein Helfrich, an older court employee recognized the potential of the young innocent girl, and took her under her wing, giving her the benefit of her life experiences. She was excellent in dealing with the higher officials and knew how to maneuver through the hierarchy of the court system.

****

When Gerda was sixteen she met the first love of her life. Dieter Beudt. He was eighteen and had an uncanny resemblance to Elvis Presley. Knowing this, he combed his hair like Elvis and turned up his collar and looked cool. Gerda was smitten but she had one big problem. Her father.

He was opposed to her having a boyfriend and placed many restrictions on her life. One of the restrictions was that she must be home by seven p.m. regardless. A few minutes late and she got her ears boxed or her face slapped. He also frequently emptied her purse on the table and looked for notes or anything that indicated a transgression in her actions. If she made a note, she wrote it in shorthand so he couldn't read it. This infuriated him and frequently resulted in some form of punishment.

Because of the restrictions, Gerda found it necessary to sneak around, hide her actions, and to tell lies about everything she did. The things she wanted to do were so typical harmless teenage activities, and the restrictions were so oppressive, that Gerda rebelled and chose to lie rather than to obey her father. She was a lousy liar and frequently forgot what story she had told her mother and gave herself away by saying something which contradicted her previous story. Her mother never got angry, but Gerda could tell from the way she looked at her that her mom was disappointed. That look was worse than a scolding.

In spite of her situation at home, she had many fun and pleasant experiences. Dieter's father had been a professor and taught school so prior to the war they belonged to the upper middle class of German society. He was drafted into the army and was killed in action. Dieter had a German Sheppard dog named Lady that Gerda loved and was loved in return. The Beudt family owned an orchard at the edge of town, so during harvest time, Dieter, Gerda and Lady spent the day in the orchard picking apples, pears and plums. For the first time in her life Gerda could eat as many apples as she wanted.

On the down side of the relationship was Gerda' requirement to be home at seven p.m. Dieter than had time to join his buddies in a *Gasthaus* and enjoy a few beers. It was rumored among the neighborhood boys that he sometimes had girl friends that Gerda knew nothing about. Ignorance is bliss, and she and Dieter dated and spent a lot of time together for the next three years. He completed an apprenticeship as a cabinet maker and made some beautiful wood items. Gerda still has a jewelry box Dieter made for her birthday. It is quite beautiful.

They had to plan their dates around her father's work schedule. When he worked nights, they could cheat a little and she could come home a little later. They also had to avoid Ludwig seeing them when they were together because he disapproved of the relationship.

One day they were in a city park and found a little kitten. Gerda immediately picked it up. The cat had other ideas and scratched her arm in several places. The scratches healed very slowly, but finally disappeared. A few days later she started developing boils on her back. A boil is like a giant pimple and very, very painful. She had to have a doctor lance the boils to drain the puss. She nearly fainted from the pain.

Gerda was in many ways rather naïve and held a distorted view of how the world functioned and about the inequalities of life. She and Dieter frequently held different views and they argued about almost everything. As she developed her career at the court, she began to see how society was divided into social levels and she liked the level in which the judges and lawyers moved, and disliked the level where her family and also Dieter lived. This added additional stress to their relationship, and gradually it came to an end.

At the court Gerda continued to grow professionally and in her world view. She still believed in the goodness of man and in the court system to provide equal justice for all. She had many interesting discussions with one of the judges about how the law really worked. The court must always uphold the law even when it appeared to be hurtful to some people. Emotions had no place in deciding the law.

She worked directly for Doctor Pullman, who was a very particular and pedantic man. He believed that the only way to do something was to do it to perfection. This suited Gerda because she shared his views on this matter. He was a true gentleman and was never rude of condescending in his treatment of her. When he pointed out an error in her work he was always gentle in the way he asked her about it.

Here again, when Doctor Pullman wanted to dictate a letter Gerda would pick up her typewriter and carry it into his office where she typed his dictation directly into the machine. Usually when he summoned her he would carry her typewriter for her. Gerda enjoyed working with him, however, most of the other recorders did not. They couldn't stand his pedantic quest for perfection. Gerda liked it.

It was common in Germany that every business or organization had an annual outing called a *"Betriebsausflug"* or company picnic. Not long after starting at the court she went on the company outing. In the evening, there was dinner and then dancing. One of the younger judges, Doctor Ortenburger asked her to dance and she gladly did so. Later when they boarded the bus for return to *Wiesbaden* it just happened that Gerda ended up sitting next to Doctor Ortenburger. In the conversation that followed he informed her that he had noticed her at work and was impressed by her professionalism. She had her hand on the seat in front of her. He looked at her hand and told her that she had very beautiful hands. Gerda was speechless. This was the start of her second true love.

They started dating and for the next couple of years she was moving within the upper crust of society. Gerda enjoyed the conversations and the intelligent discussions of politics, society, etc. There was, however, a darker side to this part of society. All of the men had graduated from a university and held the title of doctor. They tended to look down on folks with less education and were sometimes very harsh in their critique. One in particular was married to a woman who had not attended a university. He was often very rude to her telling her that she could not possible know anything about the subject, and that she should keep her misguided opinions to herself. This disturbed Gerda because she thought that he felt and even said the same about her. She was not certain of how many of their friends thought the same way.

Dr. Ortenburger was never rude to her and he never talked down to her. He treated her opinion as equal to his. He never raised his voice towards her.

Ludwig approved of this relationship. To have a judge in the family was beyond his wildest imagination. Then some damn American appeared on the scene and everything changed.

Lyle E. Herbaugh

CHAPTER NINE

THE AMERICAN

I arrived in Wiesbaden in October 1959 and checked in at Lindsey Air Station, situated in the heart of Wiesbaden. One week after arriving, I decided to visit Gerda' mother whom I had met in Mount Vernon in 1956, when she was visiting Irmgard and Glen. On Sunday about 2 p.m. I arrived at her door. Gerda was not home, so I spent a couple of hours looking at pictures from Elisabeth's American trip.

Ludwig left the apartment and walked several blocks and brought his brother Willie, who spoke good English, back with him. This helped a great deal and we did some serious visiting. At around 5 p.m. I decided to end the visit and leave. Uncle Willie insisted that I stay until Gerda came home. Several times I wanted to leave but Willie insisted that I stay. I stayed.

Around 11 p.m. Gerda came home and we were introduced. I stayed long enough to ask her to show me the town, and she agreed. To say that she was smitten would be a gross exaggeration. I was always well dressed and that day was no different. She did notice that fact.

On the following weekend, I got tickets to the opera and we attended a performance of "Die *Fledermaus*" (the Bat). Afterwards we had dinner and I walked her home. For some reason, we saw a lot of each other. She agreed to help me with my German and evenings we would practice my vocabulary words. Gerda had studied English for five years in school, so she knew a lot of words, but had no actual experience in speaking the language.

Whenever we went out we walked. I didn't own a car, but I offered to take a taxi. She always insisted that we walk even in the snow and cold of winter.

Our relationship continued to solidify, and I was invited to attend the Christmas Eve festivities with her family. It was a typical Christmas with food, exchange of gifts and real live candles on the tree. Gerda assured me that it was safe and they had been doing it for years with no problems. About five minutes after lighting the candles one was too close to a branch and it ignited. I had been sitting on pins and needles the whole time, so I immediately got up and blew out the flames. We then blew out all of the remaining candles, much to my relief.

Gerda was planning to spend a weekend at her sister's in Frankfurt and invited me to go with her. I was thrilled to say yes. I had already learned a lot of German words so I was able to keep up with the conversation with a lot of help from Gerda. She was very patient with me and helped me whenever I got stumped.

In February of 1960 Gerda went on a ski vacation in Austria. She was gone for two weeks. She took ski lessons and did quite well but she kept thinking about home and what was going to happen next. When she returned, the first evening I went to her apartment and she surprised me with some good news. She said "I am pregnant." I was thrilled and immediately told her so. She had watched my face and my reactions and if I had hesitated or showed the slightest doubt, she would have never married me.

The next problem was for us to decide the next step and tell her parents what was going on. She knew that her father would be outraged and would possibly become violent. She was right. As soon as I left that evening he started accusing her of being a whore and worthless, then he slapped her twice and threw her out. She was alone with nowhere to go. I was on the base and there was no way of notifying me. She went to a woman she knew from work and asked if she could spend the night. She of course said yes.

The next evening when I arrived at her place I was met by Karin, the neighbor girl who told me what had happened and that Gerda was waiting for me in one of the city parks. I went there as fast as I could and found her sitting on a park bench, all alone and frightened. I could tell that she was miserable. Her life had suddenly taken a horrible turn, and she had no idea what to do next. Nor did I.

Put yourself in her place for a moment. She was homeless, pregnant, and dependent on a foreigner whom she hardly knew. She knew me, but with our limited communication skills we didn't really know each other. She didn't want to get married but knew that she had to. Society did not look favorably on children born out of wedlock. She did not want to have a bastard child.

Frau Schuler agreed that she could use her spare room for a while, until we could make other arrangements.

At work, a German secretary Wiltrude Anschau and a young airman, Bill Heinemann were planning to marry. I introduced Gerda to them, and we worked out a plan. In Germany, it took nine months to complete the required background checks, and other red tape requirements to marry. We could bypass all of this if we went to Switzerland to get married. The application required our unit commander to sign the request, and the approval of Switzerland. The process took only two weeks.

Our commander wanted to meet Gerda before he would sign the request. I brought Gerda onto the base and the four of us met with Colonel Bane. He wanted to know our reason for choosing Basel Switzerland and not going through the normal German procedures. When I explained the family history and that I had known her mother since 1956, and that Gerda was pregnant, he signed. He thanked me for doing the right thing.

We had approval and an appointment with the city of Basel Switzerland to be married. We now had to figure out how to get there. Train tickets were more money than we had, so an officer at work loaned us his old car. It was not a great car, but it ran and he was sure it would make it to Basel and back. Things were coming together and Gerda relaxed a little. She was still not happy with everything that was happening, but it was a little better for her.

During the trip to Basel, Trudy and Gerda sat in the back seat and talked in German. Gerda asked Trudy if I was smart, and trustworthy, and what sort of moral character I had. She felt she was going to marry a man she knew almost nothing about, and she was confused and concerned.

Wiltrude (Trudy) had made reservations at the Hotel Metropole in Basel. We arrived the day before our appointment and did the last-minute things. The women went to the beauty shop to have their hair done. Gerda's maiden name is Boucher, which is French, so the beautician spoke to her in French. When she found that Gerda was German she switched to Swiss German, which is so different from the German spoken in Wiesbaden, that she still didn't understand. Bill and I just wasted time while the women took care of the important things.

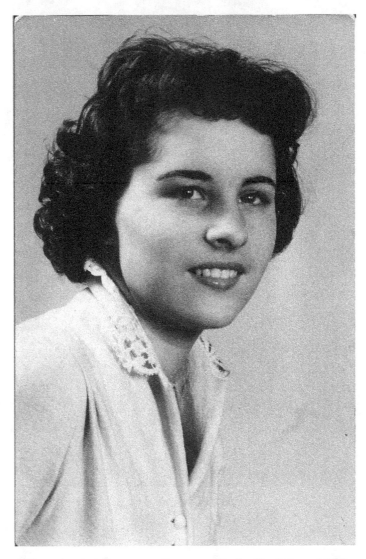

The picture I saw at Irmgard's in October 1959.

Our wedding day.

Our wedding night after wine and fruit salad.

The next morning, we arrived at the office of the magistrate who would perform the ceremony. They asked us if we wanted the marriage done in English or German. We chose English. We were ushered into the chamber where a large high desk was situated. In front of the desk facing it were four very large chairs. The door of the chamber was about four inches thick and fifteen feet high. In spite of its size it opened easily and silently. We were awe struck.

The ceremony proceeded in English, however, the official's accent was so heavy none of us could understand what he said. We did understand the instruction to say "I do" at the right place and we made it through. Ever since then, whenever we have a disagreement one of us will remind the other that "The man in Switzerland said", whatever point we want to support. It always ends with a laugh, and if there is tension in the air, it is immediately dispelled.

We were married. After paying the appropriate fees we signed a giant book with beautiful works of art and gold printing on each page. Our simple signatures looked like an abomination of such a wonderful book. We left Basel heading for the city of Lucerne.

We got rooms in the Hotel *Schluessel* (The Key), where we stayed for the next two days. We were the only people in the hotel so we had the entire staff for ourselves. We told them that we were just married and that this was our wedding night. They asked us if they could prepare a special wedding dinner for us, and of course, we said yes.

Neither of us remember what they prepared, but we both know it was fantastic. They served us a fresh fruit salad for desert. It contained so much brandy that we all got a little drunk. They had served a fantastic red wine with dinner and the combination of wine, fruit salad, and after dinner brandy, we were all feeling no pain. We retired for the night.

The next morning Gerda and I went to the dining room for breakfast. A few minutes later Bill appeared, but Trudy was nowhere to be found. During the night, they had broken the bed frame and the mattress and springs came crashing down. After assuring the staff that they were ok, they spent the rest of the night on the floor. Trudy was so embarrassed that she never did come down for breakfast.

We spent the day playing tourist, including a boat ride on lake Lucerne. The ride lasted several hours but the scenery was fantastic. Gerda was suffering from wedding remorse. She had not wanted to marry, and was very unhappy that she had to. She avoided me where and when possible. I would find her sitting alone in a corner of the boat, and when I joined her, she immediately got up and left, leaving me there wondering what the hell I had done. She was thinking the same thing, and it was the lowest point in her young life. I never saw her cry, and I don't know if she did, but I knew she was terribly unhappy.

That night Bill and Trudy broke the bed again. When we checked out Trudy went straight to the car so that she would not have to face the hotel owners. Bill, on the other hand, strutted around like a proud peacock. Gerda certainly took Trudy's position on the issue. I attempted to stay neutral.

We left Lucerne and drove to a small lake in the middle of the Black Forest of Southern Germany, called The *Titisee*. We got rooms in a small hotel right on the lake. It was about a four-hour drive from Lucerne. When we arrived, I got out of the car and walked to the other side of another car, and passed wind. Gerda heard it and she glared at me. She didn't say anything; in fact, she didn't say anything to me for two days. She went to the room and stayed there. Bill and Trudy rented a boat and went rowing on the lake. I sat on a bench by a walkway looking out over the lake. I could hear Bill and Trudy laughing and having a wonderful time. I sat there wondering what sort of hell I was in for. What had I done?

Gerda's father liked to play tricks on folks with farts. He would stand beside a lady on the street, rip one off and then declare in a loud voice that she should be ashamed of herself. Gerda hated that so strongly that my little gas expulsion had set her off. She disliked her father and his crude actions and was afraid that she had married someone just as crude and vulgar as he.

While dating the Judge, they moved in a social circle where everyone was cultured, educated, and refined. They would never pass wind under any circumstances. She did not like living in the social level of the proletariat, and loved what she perceived as the better upper level of society.

She suddenly found herself married to a farting proletariat. She was horrified.

That evening the three of us gathered in the dining room. I went to the room to see if Gerda was coming down for dinner. She was not, and made it very clear by her refusal to speak to me. I ate something and asked the waiter to prepare a sandwich for Gerda to take to the room with me. Unknown to me, years before, Gerda had eaten rancid butter at a friend's house and could not stand the taste of butter. There was butter on the sandwich. She blew her top. Not only did she speak to me, she chewed my butt for bringing her a sandwich with butter on it.

We both lie there not speaking until we fell asleep. It was the worst night of both of our lives.

Chapter Ten

STARTING A FAMILY

After returning to Wiesbaden, we moved into an apartment in a very nice part of town. The street was lined with huge old buildings which had one day been the home of the wealthy, but after the war, were converted to apartments. Ours was on the third or top floor, where we shared the place with an older woman who had been widowed by the war. The toilet was in the hallway and the kitchen was on one side and the living space was on the other side. The bathtub was in the kitchen area. It sounds terrible, but it was a rather nice apartment at the time. Even fifteen years after the war, living space was scarce and a complete apartment was rare.

Gerda returned to work and found a changed atmosphere. When she was dating the judge, she was treated with kid gloves, but when word got out that she was married to an American, things changed. Only women with loose moral character married *Amis* as Americans were known. Some of the men let her know that if they had known what kind of person she was, they would have made a move for her affection. She hated it. She lived in a state of shame and couldn't wait to get out of there. She quit her job.

Gerda then cashed out her social security deposits and we used the money to buy some furniture. Beds and some other furniture came with the apartment, but we needed some lamps, a sofa and living room chairs. We also bought some nice curtains for the living room windows and the place started to look and smell like home.

When Gerda knew that her father was working she would visit her mother or her mother came to our place. She cared a great deal for her mother and this love of her mother and dislike of her father would play a big part in our future lives. Elisabeth begged us to forgive Ludwig for what he had done and to make amends and accept him into our lives. I swore I would never talk to the man again, but to please her mother Gerda said she would, and to please Gerda, I supported her decision. We invited them over for Sunday dinner. The atmosphere was charged, but the day passed without incident. He never apologized, but he made jokes and tried to normalize things. Gerda was relieved when the day was over. It had been a struggle for her, but she had buried her feelings and accepted the situation. She somehow realized that the situation had changed. She was married and had a man in her life, which freed her from the influence of her father. She was free to live her own life.

Our relationship steadily improved. Her parents bought a new TV and gave us their old black-and-white one. I bought a small record player and a radio so we were now living comfortably. We read a lot, and spent many evenings sitting together reading. Gerda wanted to talk but my limited German and her school English didn't allow us to say what we were feeling. I know that she was lonesome and felt isolated and alone. She never complained to me or I didn't understand her if she did.

I did all of the grocery shopping in the Military Commissary. It was much cheaper than the German stores so it made sense. Gerda made a menu for the week and then made a list of everything we needed and I would go shopping. She, for some reason, did not want to go to the commissary.

My cousin, Caryl Ann, whom I loved and respected visited Europe and spent a week with us. During that time, I complained to her about Gerda's lack of English skill. Caryl Ann blew up and literally shouted at me.

"What gives you the right to complain about her English. Can you speak fluent German? This is her home country and you are the foreigner so why don't you learn German. It is time you do the right thing and learn her language."

She was right and I knew it. Following her visit Gerda and I agreed that we would only speak German until I could speak it fluently. We did, and within a year my German was pretty good and in two years I could speak and understand with native language proficiency. It was the right thing to do, and I am so glad that Caryl Ann made me see the light.

Gerda's pregnancy developed normally. She went to the U.S. Air Force Hospital in Wiesbaden for her prenatal care. A number of women who were all pregnant gathered for their appointments at the same time. I don't think they ever saw a doctor, but were cared for by a registered nurse. During one of her first visits the nurse opened the session by asking "May I have your attention please?" Gerda looked in her purse and said, "I am sorry. I didn't bring one." Everyone laughed.

As my German improved so did our relationship. I began to understand the cultural differences, and why Gerda did and said some of the things she did. She also began to understand me and we both realized that we really did care for each other, and that things were going to be all right.

Our apartment was located on a hill overlooking the *Kurpark* in downtown Wiesbaden. Every Saturday evening during the summer months they had a band playing and around 10 p.m. there was fireworks. At first Gerda didn't like them, because the loud explosions reminded her of the war and brought back some frightening memories. They were very loud for us because the hill and the building placed our apartment windows at the same level as the fireworks when they exploded. The noise was sometimes so loud it was almost painful.

During the day, I was at work and Gerda was alone. She was a member of a book club so once a month new books arrived which supplied her with new reading material. She read so fast that we had to find another source that we could afford. We went to the Base Library and checked out books. I read two or three books a week, so we checked out as many as we could. That was when Gerda started reading English. We would select books that were easy to read and she would work her way through them. It wasn't long before she was reading English almost as fast as she could read German. I was astonished at how fast she learned.

****

The months went by and it was time for Ronald to be born. We struggled to pick a name for him. At that time, there was no way of knowing the sex of the baby, so we had to plan for both. Then we had to pick a name that meant something in both languages and cultures. I wanted to name him Wendell, but that is the German word for diaper, so that was out. We chose Ronald Lyle.

The day she went into labor I took her to the Air Force Hospital and left her at the delivery room. In 1960 the husbands were not allowed in the birthing area. We were told to go home and check in from time to time and see what was going on. For two days, she was in labor and I knew nothing about it. I called and was told that she was still in labor and not to worry. Finally, I called at about five A.M. and they told me she had just delivered, and that it was a boy. I raced to the hospital and looked through a glass door at my new son. They still wouldn't let me in to see her. It was later that afternoon that I saw her and Ronald. Gerda was exhausted but both of them were beautiful.

How this tiny 98-pound young woman could stand the pain of child birth for over two days was a wonder to me. She was essentially alone during this horrible time. I was alone when I wanted to be with her and help. It was still the stone age of medicine. To relieve the pain, she was given a spinal block, and told not to stand up for 24 hours and to lie flat in bed. A few hours later a German nurse came in and told her to get up. I think the nurse got her training in *Auschwitz*, because she had no feelings or concern for the patient. She was blunt and forceful, so you did what she told you to do. Because of not staying in bed, Gerda got a severe headache that lasted night and day for the entire stay in the hospital.

She stayed in the hospital for four days and during that time the nurse asked her if she had a bowel movement. Gerda had no idea what that meant and so she always said yes. She wondered what was so important about a bowl and why would she move it. She never asked me what it meant so I was no help.

When she was released I took her to her mother's place. Elisabeth took one look at her and knew what was wrong. Gerda had not passed anything for five days and needed help. She hurried to the drug store and got a strong laxative suppository. It worked. After getting cleaned up, Gerda slept for many hours.

Prior to leaving the hospital they had told her how to mix formula and to take care of the baby. It was believed that it was better to bottle feed a baby and not to breast feed them. Gerda was so sick that she didn't understand what she was told. Later that day I went to the hospital and picked up the information we needed. I had already bought bottles and a sterilizer so we were almost prepared. I got the formula mix in the commissary and fed the baby. We had everything we needed for the baby, so that was no problem for me.

The next day Gerda, Ronald and I were alone in our home. Gerda had no idea how Americans dressed a baby, so most of the things I had bought in the Base Exchange were different. I had learned about baby care by babysitting my niece Fordell, so I knew how to do most things. I showed Gerda and in a couple of days she was working like an old pro.

We did not own a washing machine so Gerda placed the cloth diapers in a large pot and boiled them on the kitchen stove to get them clean. Then she carried the pot to the bathtub and poured them in where she rinsed them and hung them on a stand to dry. It was a lot of work but Gerda thought it was normal because that is the way her mother had done it.

There were many things that wives did for their men in those days. When we first married Gerda would shine my shoes every evening. I told her that she did not need to do that because I could shine my own shoes. She always brushed my uniform coat and pants when I got home and hung them up so they could air out. I told her she didn't have to do that and she stopped. She was a fast learner.

Ron was a crier and every night when we put him down for the night he would cry. He was fed, his diaper was dry and when you picked him up he smiled. Back into his bed and he cried. He did that for about a month, and then started sleeping normally.

For the next several months I went to work every day and Gerda stayed home and cared for Ron. She cleaned the house every day, prepared the evening meal, washed the baby clothes and read. She was alone most of the time, and I think quite lonely. She never complained to me and I was young and ignorant and insensitive to her needs.

When Ronald was about nine months old, we decided to take a vacation in Austria. Elizabeth agreed to take care of Ron and we were free to go. It was a time to heal and to grow close to each other. It was the honeymoon we had not had. We had a wonderful two weeks and returned to our normal life renewed and I think in love with each other for the first time. We finally knew each other and we liked what we found.

Office Christmas party, 1961.

After returning from Austria and settling back into the routine, I became ill. On Saturday, we had taken *Mutti* (Elisabeth) out in the country and had a picnic near some woods. It was a pleasant day, but I had the misfortune of being bitten by a tick. The following Monday I woke up with a severe headache. I don't normally have headaches so I went on Sick Call at the Air Force Hospital. After examining me the doctor admitted me to the hospital for observation. During the day and night my headache worsened. The following morning a neurosurgeon looked at me and during the examination he found that I had no reflexes in either leg. My neck was so stiff that I could not lower my chin to my chest. It felt like there was a rope tied to my head pulling it backwards. When I told the doctor he immediately ordered a lumbar puncture and removed some spinal fluid. That relieved the pressure and my headache stopped. Within a few minutes, I fell into a coma where I remained for the next seven days. I had Bacterial Spinal Meningitis and was moved into the isolation ward.

Poor Gerda. I had always told her that if someone in uniform came calling when I was at work, something was wrong and it was probably not good news they were bringing. The day I was hospitalized my boss and a German secretary rang the doorbell. Gerda knew in an instant that I was dead, or at least in terrible shape. When they had explained everything to her, they asked if there was anything they could do to help. She bravely said no. Wrong answer.

We had left the baby stroller in the car and it was parked at the hospital. The car keys were with my possessions at the hospital and I was in a coma. Ron was a heavy (fat) little guy and it was a chore for Gerda to carry him. He didn't start walking until he was almost two, so she had to carry him. She left him at her mother's and came to the hospital to see me. Before she could enter my room, she had to put on a robe, gloves and a mask. She was instructed to not touch me under any circumstances. She was so upset by the situation that she didn't understand anything they told her so she had no idea what was wrong with me. When she got to her parent's place to pick up Ron all she could tell them was that I was very sick.

She called my office and one of the Airmen went to the hospital with her and retrieved the car keys and got the stroller for her. At least now she could manage to get around with Ron. I woke from the coma after a week and then stayed in the hospital for another week to recover my strengths. It is almost a miracle, that I did not suffer any ill effects from the meningitis. From the moment, I awoke I was pain free and symptom free. I was just tired.

****

I had been in Germany for two years when we were informed that my unit would be moving from the downtown location to Wiesbaden Air Base a few miles outside of town. At the same time the landlord sold the building we were living in, and we were notified that we must move. It all came together and Gerda was introduced to her first move.

I already knew that she was organized, but the first move showed me just how much she could do.

We found an apartment in a little town a few miles from the air base. *Bischofsheim* was a small German town in a farming community. It was quiet and peaceful, but was very poor. Many of the streets and houses were in need of repair and some war damage was not yet repaired. Our apartment was on the top floor of a two-story building. A German family lived below us on the ground floor. They had a little girl who was the same age as Ronald, and they played together sometimes.

Once again, the kitchen and bathroom were on one side of the hall and the living areas on the other. The kitchen had a gas stove with a coal burning section to provide heat. The living room had an oil-fired stove with a tank on the back which had to be filled every day. Oil was stored in a shed by the house in a 50-gallon drum. Everyday Gerda would fill a one gallon can with oil and fill the tank on the stove. She was extra careful not to spill any heating oil, because it was hard to clean up and it smelled bad.

Every day the coal stove in the kitchen/bathroom had to have the ashes removed and coal added to keep the place warm. Gerda assumed responsibility for all of the things around the house and caring for Ronald. I thought it was great and let her do it. We still didn't have a washing machine so she continued to cook the laundry on the kitchen stove and rinse it in the bathtub.

In spite of all the things she did she was always finished before noon, and had the rest of the day to read and care for Ron.

My job remained the same after the move, but Gerda's tasks increased. We settled into the new routine. About a year before we moved, I bought our first new car. We paid $1200 which came to $25 a month.

Every Saturday and Sunday we visited Gerda's parents. Elisabeth made a yeast cake with *streusel* on top which was to die for. I ate cake like a madman each weekend. *Mutti* also made many other cakes and I found all of them to be delicious. She had long since decided I was a keeper and was delighted when I liked her cakes and showed my appreciation. The fact that her mother loved me meant a lot to Gerda. She tolerated her father but the air was frequently charged when they were together. No open fights, but the air seemed to crackle with static.

One evening we were watching television when Gerda raised the question: "How do you feel about having another baby?" I was delighted with the idea and a month later Gerda was pregnant.

This pregnancy went like a textbook example. Limited morning sickness, moderate weight gain, and overall a model pregnancy. Once again, she received her prenatal care at the Air Force Hospital in Wiesbaden. This time she knew what to ask and it made things much easier. Gerda continued to fill the oil stove and service the coal stove in the kitchen. Every day she faithfully fulfilled what she perceived to be her duties.

The time finally arrived when she went into labor. Of course, it was during the day when I was at work and she was alone. We did not have a telephone in those days because the German infrastructure was way behind the U.S. due to having been totally destroyed during the war. It was another 10 years before we got our first phone. It was necessary for Gerda to dress Ronald and put him in the stroller, then walk five blocks to the nearest pay phone. But before she could do that she felt that she needed to prepare the house so I would be comfortable and warm. She filled both the oil stove and the coal stove in between contractions. I got the call and immediately drove home. Gerda was waiting for me with Ron in the stroller and her bag packed. By the time we got to the hospital her contractions were only five minutes apart. We rushed her to the birthing center where she was met by a rotund African American nurse who wrapped her arms around Gerda and told her she would take care of her, and she should just go ahead and have that baby.

It was late afternoon when I delivered her to the hospital so I took Ron to *Mutti's* where he could stay overnight. I ate dinner and then I went back to the hospital to see if anything was happening. Since her contractions were so close together I thought maybe the baby would be born any moment. I was right. When I arrived at the hospital there was another healthy baby boy waiting for me. Shift change had occurred and the nurse who had greeted her told her, "Honey, I told you I would take care of you and I'm not going to leave you until you have that baby." She stayed right there holding Gerda's hand and giving her encouragement.

I went back to Gerda's parents to give them the news. When I started home, I asked Ron if he wanted to stay with

Oma or come home with me. He wanted to be with me, so I packed his things and took him with me.

It was the start of a record cold winter. Gerald was born on November 19, 1962 and Gerda stayed four days in the Hospital. I don't remember the dates, but we celebrated Thanksgiving while they were in the hospital. On November 21, it started snowing and Winter was on its way. We did not see the ground until the following April. The Winter was one of the coldest on record. It was so cold that the Rhine River froze over (see above picture) and all shipping stopped. Most of the coal and oil that was used for heat in much of Germany was suddenly not available. The limited supply was given only to the German customers. We Americans could not buy any, no matter how much money we had.

As luck would have it, during the Summer I had purchased a quantity of coal and had it stored in the cellar of the house. It was enough to last the entire winter, but we could not buy heating oil so we had no way of heating the living rooms and bed rooms. With a two-year-old and an infant to care for and no heat in the main part of the house, what were we going to do.

The Air Force came to the rescue. They brought in heating oil from the states and sold it to us who needed it. I removed the backseat of the car, bought several five-gallon gas cans and every few days made the trip and picked up enough oil for a week. The car always smelled of heating oil, but we managed. As it turned out, we spent less money on heating that winter than we did when we bought it on the German economy.

Once again Gerda excelled. With the weather below zero for weeks on end, she made her daily trips to the cellar and to the oil cans and filled the stoves to keep the family warm. This was in addition to caring for a two-year-old and for an infant, cooking, cleaning the house and doing the laundry. She proved again how organized she is and somehow made it look easy. It was not, but she is good at everything she does.

CHAPTER ELEVEN

USA HERE WE COME
SEPTEMBER 1963

After four years in Germany my tour was coming to an end. I was not happy working in personnel and wanted a change in career field. Computers had just been fielded in a major air defense system across the United States and Canada. Maintenance and operation of the computers was being transferred to Air Force personnel, and they were looking for people with the right intelligence and aptitudes for computers. I took a test and passed. I was accepted and scheduled to attend a one year (52 week) course at Keesler Air Force Base, in Biloxi, Mississippi.

In preparation for entering the United States, Gerda completed a mountain of paperwork for both the German and U.S. officials. Finally, she had an interview with an official in the American Consulate. During the interview, she had to confirm that she was not and had never been a prostitute. She was granted a visa followed in a few weeks by a Green Card. She was ready to leave Germany.

This would be our first major move where the packers would come to the house and pack everything we owned in boxes and then in shipping crates and take them away. We were left with the clothes on our back and whatever we had packed in our suit cases.

We spent the final few days living with Gerda's parents. They didn't have enough room for us to sleep so we went across the hall and spent the nights with Karl Heinz and Renata Burkhardt. It was inconvenient but it worked. Soon it was time to say goodbye.

This was a very difficult goodbye for Gerda. She loved her mother very much and because of this love, much of how we had lived our lives since we married was to please Elisabeth. In addition to the fear that we might never see her again was a sense of peace. She would miss her mother, but for the first time in her life she would be free of her father's dominance. The years of punishment for perceived transgressions, the fear, the shouting, and the physical and mental abuse, were all being left behind. She would be free at last.

Before leaving Germany, we had ordered a new car to be delivered to Trenton New Jersey. It would be waiting for us at the dealership when we arrived. It was a silver Nash Rambler Classic with red interior and upholstery. We flew from Rhine-Main Air Base near Frankfurt to McGuire Air Base near Trenton, on a Military charter plane. We cleared customs and immigration and took a taxi to the car dealership where our beautiful new car was waiting as promised. We had registered it through the factory located in Wisconsin so it had Wisconsin plates. Our final destination was the state of Mississippi and we had no idea how serious it would become that we had Wisconsin plates on our car.

We left the dealership around noon and found our way to the Pennsylvania Turnpike. In route, I asked Gerda to look for a place where we could get some lunch. She didn't see any but I noticed a couple of cafes and we finally stopped and had lunch. She had seen several cafes but in Germany a café is where you buy cake and coffee, not lunch. It was her first lesson in how different words mean different things in different countries.

We drove right straight through to Chicago where we spent the night with My Aunt Thelma. Gerda was a nervous wreck by the time we got there. She was about to meet one of my favorite people in the world. We didn't know it but my Aunt Florence was there with her young daughter Paige, so Gerda got to meet two of my most loved aunts. They treated her as if she was a queen and made her feel so welcome that she felt right at home in just a few minutes. We relaxed.

The next morning, we headed west. From Chicago to Mount Vernon there were no more four lane highways. The interstate system was just being built but on the route we drove there was none. Gerda held a Rand McNally road atlas on her lap and guided me telling me where to turn and onto what road. It was a great way to learn the USA. She also opened Gerda's Deli in the front seat. Ronald was almost three and Gerald was nine months old. Car seats had not been developed yet, so Ron sat in the back seat and Gerald lay there most of the time.

Our approach to travel was to start early in the morning. We would take the sleeping boys and lay them in the back seat, cover them with a blanket and let them sleep while we drove. Around eight a.m. we would stop for breakfast. We would change diapers, change from pajamas to clothes for the day and then go to a restaurant and eat.

Next step was to find a grocery store and replenish Gerda's deli with provisions for the day. Around noon we stopped at the city park of some small town and had a picnic. Ron could run around and burn off some energy, and I could take a short nap, then it was down the road again. In the early evening after having traveled for twelve hours we would find a motel for the night.

The early morning time was the best time of the day. It was cool and the wild life was out in profusion. In Wyoming, we saw deer, elk and antelope by the thousands. Anywhere there was water to drink the antelope gathered. It was a thrill for Gerda, and for me. As we drove from one small town to the next Gerda made a point of looking for some distinguishing feature of the towns. The highway went right through the center of every town so she got to see America as it was, and she loved it.

Years later Gerda would meet some young airman who would respond to her question: "Where are you from?" with oh some little town in Iowa. When asked for the name of the town they would respond. Many times, she told the kid: "Oh yes, that is a nice town. The little city park is nice and there is a grocery store on the corner of third street right across from the Conoco gas station." It was priceless to see the expression on their faces when this German woman knew all about their little home town. They immediately loved her.

We were driving on highway 20 across northern Nebraska when we got into a severe thunder storm. We watched it form but there was nothing we could do but press on. When we entered the storm, it turned as dark as night. Lightning bolts were flashing all around us. The rain was coming down so hard the wipers couldn't keep up. I slowed down and tried to stay on the road. Gerda was fascinated by the storm but had no idea how dangerous it was. We were in the rolling hills of Nebraska and I feared that the next low spot could be filled with water from a flash flood.

I was terrified that we could drive right into a tornado. It was so dark and the visibility was so low that I would have been right in the center of a tornado before I could see it. I drove on. We came out the West side of the storm and the sun was suddenly shining and the day was very pleasant. I was exhausted from the stress of driving through the storm. We arrived in Gordon, Nebraska and stopped at the first motel we found. It was late afternoon.

We asked the lady in the front office about a good place to eat. She recommended a small café just a block away. I don't remember what we ate, but the portions were huge. We were in the middle of dinner when a real live cowboy walked in. He wore a western hat, jeans and a beautiful shirt with mother-of-pearl snaps. Gerda saw him walk in and she almost choked on her French fries. She poked me in the side and said: "Is that a real cowboy? Isn't he gorgeous." Her first real cowboy, and she was dumbstruck. The next morning, we were back on the road.

After driving for seven days we arrived in Mount Vernon, Washington. Our first stop was at Glen and Irmgard's place. After the greetings were over we relaxed for an hour. I called Mom and Dad and told them we were on our way out to see them. This was the first time for my parents to meet their daughter-in-law and their two grandsons.

It was an emotional time for everyone, especially my parents. First their new daughter-in-law spoke English with an accent, their grandson spoke only German and everything was different. Their youngest son had grown into a man who had confidence and who could switch between German and English with ease. They were very proud of him. For Gerda, everything was new. Irmgard told her before we left her place that she

75

should be ready to get hugged, because the Herbaugh family hugged a lot. She did not like public displays of affection, so hugging was not something with which she was comfortable. Everyone survived and over the next two weeks we all grew to love each other.

While we were in Mount Vernon, Glen built a bench that fit in the backseat of the car. It fit between the front and back seats. The top was level with the back seat, making the entire back seat area one flat surface. We spread a heavy quilt over the bench and seat, and the boys had a large area to lie, sleep, play and survive the traveling. Irmgard had a large basket that was big enough for Gerald to sleep in, which fit in the backseat. When we left for Mississippi small things that had just been scattered around the car were stored under the bench. Gerald had a place to sleep, and Ronald had space to move around. Gerda retained her deli in the front seat.

The trip to Mississippi was much like the trip from New Jersey. Early start, stops for breakfast and lunch and toilet breaks. As we traveled south the days got hotter. We were in northern Texas on the hottest day of the year. It was 97 degrees in the shade. We stopped in a roadside park for lunch. Gerda was sitting at a picnic table with Gerald on her lap. She was feeding him when she cried out very loud, "There is an ant on my foot and it's biting me." I laughed and looked at her foot. She had stepped on a fire ant nest and they didn't like it. I took Gerald and she quickly brushed the ants off of her foot, but it was too late. One of them had bitten her and it hurt. Within an hour her leg was swollen from her foot to her knee. It was Sunday and I had no idea what to do. We stopped at the next town and I found a drug store that was open. The pharmacist gave us something to apply to the leg and some pain meds. The next morning her leg was fine, but the memory of the pain would remain for years.

CHAPTER TWELVE

LIFE IN THE STATES
SEPTEMBER 1963 TO JULY 1966

When we arrived in Louisiana Gerda was repulsed by the hanging moss that hung from every tree. Not just in swampy areas, but along the road. It was everywhere. I found it interesting but she was repulsed. As we drove through the farmland we began to see little rundown shacks with dirt floors. At every house were black children playing. It was the worst poverty we had ever seen.

We needed gas so I pulled into the first station I came to. A black man came out and filled the tank for me. Ronald and I both needed to use the restroom so we did. I had no idea what we were doing. I knew the South was segregated, but I didn't know the rules, and with the freedom riders being in Mississippi trying to register blacks to vote, and with Wisconsin plates on the car, I was afraid I would do something to bring the wrath of the southern whites down on our backs.

We arrived Biloxi, Mississippi and drove onto Keesler Air Force Base. We suddenly felt safe. I reported in and was told that it would be two weeks before we could move into military housing so we should find suitable accommodations off base. We found a little motel with individual cabins to rent. We took one for two weeks. That first evening all hell broke loose which terrified Gerda and influenced our stay in Mississippi.

The little cabin we rented had two bedrooms, a living area and kitchen with a table for eating. The living room and bedrooms were all carpeted but the hallway and kitchen area had linoleum floor covering. The first night, the boys were in bed and we had settled down to watch some television. Gerda sat upright with a startled look on her face. "What's that noise? She almost whispered. I could see that she thought someone was trying to break in and was terrified. I went into the hallway and turned on the light. Walking up the hallway was the biggest roach I had ever seen in my life. It was at least four inches long and as it walked it made a scratching sound.

I turned to Gerda and told her it was only a roach. She came over and looked into the hall and screamed in German. *Mein Gott, mach es tot.* "Kill it, my God kill it." I didn't kill it but I caught it and threw it outside. In the process, we turned on the light in the kitchen and it looked like the entire room moved. There must have been a hundred roaches of all sizes and shapes on the walls, the table and the kitchen cabinets. I was upset, but I thought Gerda would lose it. She just knew that at night the roaches would crawl all over our bed and that was a terrible thought.

I lied to her, telling her that because the carpet was long shag, they could not walk on it, and that roaches cannot fly. She believed me, and the bed became her safe haven. She spent as much time as possible on the bed with the boys close to her.

During the day, the roaches were nowhere to be seen. They only came out when it was dark. The next day we went to a hardware store and she bought a hand pump sprayer and two quarts of insect spray. We used newspaper to stuff any cracks or holes we found in the entire cabin, and then saturated it with Gulf Spray. The place stunk like a chemical plant, but it took care of most of the roaches. At least it became bearable.

The following day I started school, and left the place at 5a.m. The car was parked about twenty feet from the front door, but by the time I made it to the car I was covered with mosquitoes. I got in the car and spent several minutes killing the pests. I have never seen so many mosquitoes in my life. It was terrible. You could not be outside without being attacked by swarms of mosquitoes.

It was bearable for the first week, but one day I came home from school and found Gerda standing in the living room swatting things from her legs. She knew a roach was crawling up her leg and she wanted it gone. I thought, oh God, I'm going to have to send her and the kids to Irmgard's for the year I'm in school.

I assured her that there was nothing on her and that she was safe and nothing was going to harm her. We made it through the two weeks and moved into Government Housing on the base. The Air Force sprayed the entire area every evening to control the roaches and the mosquitoes. It worked, but during the year we lived there we were constantly bombarded by the smell and effects of DDT. I don't know if it hurt us or not, we were only happy that we were free of the bugs.

We settled into a routine. I was at school from six a.m. until one p.m. and Gerda was home with the boys. We owned very little furniture, so we were provided free stuff from housing supply. We went to Sears and bought a sofa and chair as well as a television. Every morning Ronald and Gerda watched cartoons. Ronald spoke no English when we arrived, but within four weeks he talked like he had been speaking English his entire life. Gerda's English also improved rapidly. First she learned a lot from the cartoons but she was visited every day by the women in the neighborhood, and had to speak English.

As the days passed I started to notice a change in Gerda. Since we first met she had always had several nervous tics that were spontaneous. One caused her to wrinkle her nose. It happened every few minutes. One day I noticed that she was not twitching her nose at all. I didn't say anything, but I was thrilled.

She noted in the base paper that the base education office was offering a driver's education class for new drivers. Gerda called and signed up for the class. She was going to get her driver's license and gain her independence. Another wife who lived in our neighborhood also signed up. The two of them marched off to class in the evening. One evening they were returning from class and I noticed that Gerda was walking differently. She seemed completely relaxed and sure of herself in a way I had never seen before. I was anxious to know what had changed her so profoundly. Later that evening when the boys were in bed I asked her how she felt about our life in the U.S.

"I am free for the first time in my life. I am free to do anything I want to do and I don't have to fear or answer to my father."

She passed her tests and soon had a learner's permit. I drove with her several times and she drove very competently and I was sure she would make a good driver. She finished driver's school and we went down town to the state Department of Licensing and she took her drivers exam. She passed both the written and driving tests and was given an official driver's license of the State of Mississippi. Then I messed up and changed everything.

We were all in the car and she was driving. We approached a busy intersection and it appeared to me that she was going to roll right through the stop sign. I reached over and stepped on the brake and stopped the car. Her confidence evaporated in an instant. She drove for several more days and then she confessed to me: "I don't want to drive anymore. When the boys are with me I am afraid that I will get in an accident and kill us all. I can't get the image out of my mind." I made a huge mistake and told her that if she was afraid to drive, then she shouldn't drive. It was the wrong thing to say, and she stopped driving. She didn't drive again for the next ten years.

The year passed. I attended class in the mornings but had every afternoon free. The first few weeks I had to study in the afternoon, but for the rest of the year I never studied. I learned everything I needed to know in the classroom.

With the afternoons free it seemed like I was on vacation. We did what most families did when their children were small. We filled the little wading pool with water, covered all of our bodies with insect repellent and went outside and played. We went to the beach once but it was dirty and there was broken glass everywhere. The resort hotels located on the beach of course had their own private beaches which were spotlessly clean. We couldn't go there because we were not guests of the hotels.

One day several of us went into the backwoods for a picnic on a river. One of the guys brought his 38-caliber revolver and we took turns shooting at cans and targets across the river. The shots hit a high sand bank so no one was in danger. When it was Gerda's turn to shoot, we emptied the gun and showed her how to hold it, cock it and then shoot it. She practiced with an empty gun several times and then it was time for the real test. We loaded one shell in the chamber and gave her the gun. She was to shoot at a can on the other side of the river. She aimed and hit the can. She was startled by the recoil but hit the can on the very first try. We loaded another shell and she did it again. She shot several times and did an amazing job of hitting what she was shooting at. She was pleased and I was amazed.

November 22, 1963: I was at school. Several of us were standing outside during our morning break when someone who had been sitting in their car listening to the radio, came running towards the group shouting "They just shot Kennedy." I immediately went inside to the nearest phone and called Gerda and told her to turn on the TV, the president had been shot.

All of that afternoon and for the next three days we were glued to the TV. We were watching when Jack Ruby shot and killed Oswald. It was a traumatic experience to see someone shot, live on television. For Gerda it was unbelievable. She was in a new country and watched the president get killed and then the assassin gets assassinated. This is something you would read about in a murder mystery, not watch live on TV. We had seen a billboard along the freeway that said "Kill Kennedy", but we never thought someone would do it. It was a sad time for us all.

We both grew to hate Mississippi. The racial prejudice and the horrible treatment of blacks, the attitude of the people, the entire society repulsed us. The mosquitoes, roaches, other insects along with the heat and humidity made living there almost unbearable. Gerda never complained, but we did spend most of our time on base. Whenever we left the base for any reason, I hung a uniform in the back seat and put my Air Force hat in the back window, so that the locals would not mistake me for one of the freedom riders and shoot me. We could hardly wait for the school to end and we would get our next assignment. It almost ended in a disaster.

I graduated as number one in the class and selected as Honor Student. The Air Force needed instructors for the school and decided that anyone graduating in the top ten percent of the class would automatically become instructors and stay at Keesler Air Force Base for the next four years. I was selected. Before that selection was made I was given an assignment to Duluth Minnesota. We were not happy because we wanted to go to McCord Air Force Base in Tacoma, Washington. We would be close to home and Gerda would be close to her sister Irmgard. After a series of back and forth and me telling everyone that I did not want to stay in Mississippi, I was relieved from instructor duty and assigned to McCord. The day the school ended we were on the way to Washington. We had saved the bench for the back seat. We installed it, loaded the car and we headed for the northwest.

Gerda was thrilled that we were leaving the land of bugs and roaches behind. The first night we were staying the night somewhere in eastern Texas. Gerda and the boys were in bed, and I went into the bathroom to take a shower. I was just about to get in when I heard Gerda scream. I thought something horrible had happened and races naked into the bedroom. She was sitting on a chair pointing at the ceiling crying. There above the bed was a black cricket. It was one of the ugliest insects I have ever seen, but quite harmless. I caught it and put

85

it outside. It was too big to crush, so out it went. Gerda was afraid to turn out the lights for fear it might return. She had been so happy to be rid of the roaches and then this had to happen. The next day we left roach country.

The trip to Washington was much like the last one a year before. Gerda held the map and gave me directions. She opened her deli in the front seat and served up snacks, sandwiches, drinks and other delicious tidbits on demand. We saw herds of wildlife which Gerda loved. Once again she paid special attention to the little towns we passed through. She was becoming a real specialist on small town America.

We dropped our bags in Mount Vernon, dividing our evenings between Glen and Irmgard and Mom and Dad. During the day, we went to Tacoma and looked for a place to live. I had contacted the base and they told me Government housing was not available and that I should look for a place to live off-base. We found a nice two-bedroom house not far from the base and moved in. We didn't have much furniture so we accepted donations. Mom and Dad gave us an old overstuffed chair and Irmgard gave us a second overstuffed chair, and a dining room table that Glen had built years before. They also provided beds for the boys.

I still had a couple of weeks to go before I had to sign in and start work. We bought some upholstery material at a remnant store and reupholstered the chairs. I also bought some material and built a breakfast nook, a bookcase for the living room, and night stands and a chest for the bedroom. We bought new beds at Sears. By the time I reported to the base, we were all set. While I had been working on other things, Gerda had bought some unbleached muslin and sewed curtains for the whole house. Irmgard was a huge help because she had learned how to survive on very little and was able to show Gerda the things she had to learn the hard way. We were ready to start our new life. The next two years would become the best two years of our lives.

When we were house-hunting, we discovered a German Deli and Bakery not far from our new house. They had everything you could ask for. German bread baked fresh daily. German sausages and cold cuts plus a wide selection of other German items. It was a gold mine for us.

Our lives were changed. Gerda was free from her past and from her father. We had become very close and were happy and content in our married relationship. Life could not be better. The boys were a joy to be with. They played together all of the time and were never a problem.

We only stayed in the first house for a few weeks, then we found a little house in a nice neighborhood and it had a fenced in backyard. The back fence opened to a wooded area, so we did not have neighbors on all four sides. It was quiet and peaceful.

The first week I fixed the fence and bought some white paint so Gerda could paint it during the day when I was working. She put on some work clothes and went to work. As often happens she got paint on her clothes. The next day she put on fresh clothes and got paint on them, and the third day she did it again. Instead of wearing the same thing every day she soiled three outfits with paint. She has no idea what was going through her head and laughs about it all these years later.

I worked rotating shifts that worked out so that every six weeks I had four days off and then on the fifth day I went to work in the evening. We had essentially a five-day vacation every six weeks. Every six weeks we went to Mount Vernon and stayed with Irmgard and my parents.

We had a lot of fun during our visits. We got to know my parents and they grew to love Gerda and the boys. It was the only time we were able to spend quality time with my mom and dad and we all enjoyed it very much.

Glen was a fisherman and loved the Skagit River which runs through Mount Vernon. Every break he got in his building design business he spent on the river fishing. He invited Gerda to go with him one morning and she gladly accepted. We bought her a fishing license, Glen provided the gear and they were ready to go. They left the house at five a.m. and hit the river. Glen had a little boat named "The Chicken Ship" with a little cabin on it and a small stove with which to cook coffee or whatever you liked. They put their lines in the water and Glen made breakfast of bacon and eggs. After eating Gerda lie down in the cabin and waited. In a few minutes, something took her line and ran with it. She jumped up, hit her head on the ceiling and staggered out to grab her pole. Twenty minutes later she landed a twenty-seven-pound King Salmon. She was hooked and they went fishing every time we were in Mount Vernon. Glen had a fishing partner and he loved it.

When I worked the evening shift I came home around eleven and Gerda was waiting for me. Frequently she met me at the door and asked if I would like a pizza. We lived only three blocks from a pizza restaurant which made it very convenient. I called and ordered a carry-out and picked it up a few minutes later. At that time, no one delivered pizza to your door. We ate pizza and watched Jonny Carson and the Tonight Show.

She loved roasted chestnuts and a store near our house carried them when they were in season. I don't know how many times I made the trip to the store for a pound of chestnuts. One evening the clerk at the store asked me what I did with them. I told her that we simply baked them in the hoven, and when they were tender we ate them. I neglected to tell her that you had to slit the shell so steam could exit or they would explode like popcorn. The next time I came in she wanted to kill me. She said that her kitchen had chestnuts on the ceiling from the exploding nuts. I blame Gerda for that, because she never told me what she did when she baked the chestnuts.

We went on frequent hikes in nature with Glen and his family. We packed a picnic lunch of fried chicken and other delicacies and went up river in the mountains and had a fun time.

On the weeks when I worked Gerda was alone a lot. She had met a couple of German girls at the German deli and they visited often. They were at our house and Gerda was telling them that our seventh anniversary was coming up and about our plans for the event. They asked when it was and she told them that it was April 5th. They looked at each other and burst out laughing. They reminded Gerda that "Today is April 7th, and I think you missed something." She immediately called me at work and tried to fain anger when she told me that I had forgotten our anniversary. She couldn't pull it off and started laughing. We had both forgotten.

Tacoma Washington has a park and aquarium at Point Defiance. It became our favorite place to go. There was an old fort there and a children's park called Never-Never-Land. It was a series of famous nursery rhymes depicted in real life buildings and models. There was a beautiful rose garden and in the spring, it was an explosion of color in azaleas and rhododendrons. It was a magical place to be and to spend time. We went there often on my free days.

Time flew by and we had been living there for two years. I loved my work, Gerda was happy and content with her life and we planned on doing this for two more years. Because the Air Force had spent so much money on me sending me to school for a year, my assignment to McCord was fixed at four years so I was not eligible for reassignment for two more years.

I didn't care because my date of separation was coming up in April of 1966. I had taken the test with IBM and had been accepted to be hired the day after I separated from the Air Force. IBM was building the Saturn Five launch and control system in Cape Canaveral, FL and I was to be assigned there as soon as I was hired. We were both thrilled that I would be a part of the program to put a man on the moon and return him safely to earth. Life has its way of getting in the way of the best laid plans, and things didn't work out the way we planned.

January 1966 Gerda got a letter from her father. Elisabeth had suffered a massive stroke and was paralyzed on her left side. She was in the hospital and they were not sure if she would live, and if so, what the extent of her abilities would be. Gerda called me at work, and then she called her sister Irmgard. We didn't have the money to send Gerda to Germany and we had no credit. Credit cards were not in wide use then and we didn't qualify to have one. Everyone decided that Irmgard should go and help their parents through this hard time.

After a few days, Irmgard made an assessment of the situation and we all decided that I should apply for a humanitarian assignment to Germany. The Air Force had such a program but it was designed for use only within the United States. There was no provision for someone to be assigned overseas to help a foreign family. Also, the situation had to be such that it could be solved in one year. It didn't look good and Gerda was really torn by her desire to help her Mother and her need to stay with the family.

For the second time in three years I called on my old friends from my time of working in personnel and asked if there was some way to get a humanitarian assignment to Germany. I was told to put the package together and submit the request. They would see if there was anything they could do. I submitted it with little hope that it would be approved. Gerda was distraught and worried about what was going to happen to her Mother. The request was approved with the requirement that I extend my enlistment for four more years. I said yes and in June 1966 we were on our way back to Germany. My job with IBM was gone forever and my dream of working the moon project vanished. Gerda worried that I would be upset and that I would somehow resent what we did. I didn't. For me it is just another thing that one must deal with and the family welfare always came first.

CHAPTER THIRTEEN
GERMANY, SECOND TOUR
JULY 1966 TO SEPTEMBER 1972

My assignment was not to Wiesbaden but to Ramstein Air Base located about seventy miles to the west. It would have to do, but first we had to get there.

We drove across the country again, this time using the same traveling pattern we had used in the past. The boys were almost three years older so we didn't build up the back seat like we had on the trip to Mississippi. We stopped for a day in Yellowstone National Park and saw several bears and a lot of other wildlife. We arrived in Trenton New Jersey and reported to the Base from which we were to catch our flight to Germany. We would be traveling on a Military Charter flight which departed on time. We had made arrangements to have the car shipped by a commercial company to Germany. They picked up the care at McGuire AFB and delivered it to us at Ramstein a month later.

By the time we arrived, Irmgard had long since returned to Mount Vernon and Elisabeth was home from the hospital. We stayed for several days. I left Gerda and the boys in Wiesbaden and I went to Ramstein and started looking for an apartment to rent. There were not many places to be had that met the standards we were accustomed to. I finally located an apartment in a two-family home in the little town of

Kindsbach. We were in the second-floor apartment and another military family lived on the ground floor. The wife was also a German girl from Munich. She and Gerda hit it off right away.

I returned to Wiesbaden on the weekend to pick up the family and move them to Kindsbach. On Saturday afternoon Elisabeth had another stroke, and went to a hospital not far from their apartment. There she received excellent care but it was too late to reverse the paralysis on her left side.

We moved into our new home. With the furniture we shipped from Washington, and what we were issued from Base Housing Supply, we had everything we needed to sit up housekeeping. At work, I was assigned to a job where I was dealing with German workers much of the time making it necessary to speak mostly German at work.

Gerda made friends with a French woman married to an Air Force Master Sergeant who worked on the system I was going to be maintaining and who also lived in Kindsbach. We met Master Sergeant Howard Phillips and his family and everyone liked each other. They had three children, Howard Junior, and twins Michael and Helene who were the same age as Ronald. All of the children played very well together and we all became close friends. We spent a lot of time with them and later when I was on the road, they helped Gerda in many ways.

We settled into life in Kindsbach. At work, I was bored to death. Because of my German language skills, I was placed in charge of the machine shop where two German workers were employed. One did not speak English and needed a lot of supervision and guidance. I was unhappy. The system was totally different from the last computer I had worked on in Tacoma, and where I was situated, I could never learn it without attending a school. In November, I got that chance. I was selected to attend a twelve-week school in Biloxi, Mississippi. I would leave for the school on January 2, 1967.

Gerda was not pleased that I would be leaving for three months, but she recognized that without the school I was never going to be happy.

Every Christmas we picked up her parents and brought them to our house for the holidays. Both Elisabeth and Ludwig were very regimented in their life styles and we were very flexible so the contrasting ways generated some conflict between Gerda and her father. He demanded that we eat breakfast at eight am, mid-day meal at noon, coffee at four pm and the evening meal at six pm. The noon meal was the main meal of the day so Gerda had to adjust from cooking an evening meal that we were used to, and cook at noon and make sandwiches in the evening. With Ronald being in school and me working having the main meal at noon was a major adjustment. It put a lot of stress on Gerda and increased her workload a great deal.

Gerda would keep leftovers from noon and reheat it for Ron and me in the evenings. It worked but doubled the times she needed to wash dishes and clean the kitchen. It was amazing how well Gerda could adjust to the changing needs. I think she is the most organized person I have ever known. This organizational skill was needed many time during the years when I was away for work or unable to get away from work. She adjusted and did whatever was required.

This year we made a terrible mistake. I was leaving for school right after the holidays and since her parents were already there, we decided that they should stay with us while I was away at school for three months. It sounds easy, but for Gerda it turned out to be a nightmare. She and her father managed to stay out of each other's hair most of the time, but every once in a while, he would say or do something that upset her and they would have a verbal set-to. The air seemed to crackle with static electricity and things would get a little ugly. This placed a great deal of stress on Gerda that she had to deal with alone. Usually, when I was home, she could vent her frustrations with me, but I was 10,000 miles away and we did not have a telephone, so she had to deal with everything alone.

Then midway through my absence, Ronald came home with the mumps and of course, Gerda got the mumps. The German doctor came to treat Elisabeth he looked at Gerda and directed that she go to bed and take care of herself. There was no way she could to that. She had meals to cook, children to take care of and all of her normal household chores to do. Her only recourse was to tough it out, and she did.

Being separated from my family and Gerda's experience changed the direction of our lives. Our future decision to leave the military to avoid me spending a year in Viet Nam was greatly affected by the three-month separation. I vowed that I would never choose to be away from Gerda and the kids for more than a few days, ever again. I never did.

At that time in our lives I was a computer geek. I lived and breathed computers. I brought home the technical orders from work and read about the computer system for fun. I felt that I needed to know everything there was to know about the system and how information flowed from the radar set to the operator at the control consoles. I learned fast and it wasn't long before my boss discovered that I knew more about the system than anyone else at the depot where I was assigned.

The German Air Defense System was spread over all of West Germany. The U.S. Air Force was responsible for the operation and maintenance of six control sites and a depot repair facility (where I was assigned). The official policy was that if a site was out of the network because of an equipment malfunction for more than four hours, someone from the headquarters would be dispatched to help restore the system. I was selected to be that person. My first time out, I arrived at the site and we found the problem in about 30 minutes. I had very little to do with the repair but I got the credit.

The next time I was sent out the same thing happened. Again, I had little to do with the repair, but we fixed it in less than an hour and I got the credit for the rapid repair. I kept learning and got better with cach trip. Soon I had the reputation of being "mister fixit" and the boss started automatically sending me. A problem was reported and I was on my way. Sometimes I was called at the site we had just restored and told to not come home but to go to another site that was having problems. This became the norm and I was gone almost every week. I was usually home for the weekend, but I was gone a lot. Gerda was always alone with the family and with no one to talk to. Without the Phillips family, she would have gone nuts.

Frequently I would leave on Monday and return on Friday. Having eaten in restaurants for the past week I was ready for a good home cooked meal. Gerda, having been alone for the entire week, was ready to go out and eat and just get out of the house. I never let her know how I felt and we went out. It became a Sunday ritual that we walk up to a place called Schuff's. They served very large portions at very reasonable prices. Everything was cooked fresh and it was just like home cooked.

After a big meal, we would go for a walk to work off some of the excess. A frequent destination was a little lake called *Baerenloch*. There was a *kiosk* right on the edge of the lake where we would buy some ice cream for dessert. We sometimes brought stale bread and fed the ducks that made the lake their home. It was peaceful and we loved the family time. With me being gone so much, the time together as a family was precious to both Gerda and me.

The couple that lived on the ground floor of our two-family house moved into government housing on the base. We moved downstairs where the apartment was a little bit larger. A nice family moved in above us. The wife was a German girl from Southern Germany. They had a daughter who was old enough to be a babysitter for us, so if we wanted to go out some evenings our babysitter was available. After the boys were in bed and asleep she could go home. The mother then listened to see if everything was quiet below.

Saturday night became our fun night out. We joined Howard and Genette Phillips for a night of dancing at the Ramstein Non-Commissioned-Officer's Club. There was a live band performing every Saturday, and we had a lot of fun dancing and talking. Some evenings we were joined by two other couples and everyone enjoyed our evenings together. On some evenings, we would all go to one of the couple's houses for breakfast. We arrived home in the wee hours of the morning.

One evening we were all at the club dancing when a strange thing happened. Gerda and I returned to the table from dancing with someone else. We had just sat down when we looked at each other and at the same instant we asked "why are we doing this?" It suddenly wasn't fun anymore, and like so many things in life, it had run its course and we were ready to move on. That phase of our lives came to an end.

Another phase of our lives was about to come to an end. I was approaching my date of separation from the Air Force and we had to decide if I should reenlist or get out of the service. I had been serving in the Air Force for 14 years and could retire in six more years. Viet Nam was raging in 1969 and most of my co-workers were returning to the U.S. and in less than a year they were in Viet Nam. We had spent three months apart and the idea of me being gone for a year did not appeal to either of us. Gerda was not as worried about the year apart as she was about the possibility that I could be killed and never come home to the family. We spent many hours discussing all the pros and cons of the issue and together we decided that I should leave the service and find a job in the civilian world.

The issue was complicated by the condition of Elisabeth. Gerda did not want to leave her mother again with her sitting on the sofa unable to walk without assistance and needing our emotional support. Gerda knew that there were some civilian jobs in the system I was working on and thought it would be perfect if I could get one of the positions. I would not be doing actual maintenance but would be training the enlisted personnel to do the maintenance. After much discussion, I agreed that I would try and find one, but in the mean time I would look for other jobs not connected with the military. She reluctantly agreed. In her mind a Government job meant job security and a pension in old age. Having had nothing in and after the war, this feeling of security a Government job provided was very important to her.

Several jobs came open in the system and with my reputation as "Mr. Fixit" the people doing the hiring wanted me. There was only one problem, all of the jobs were for Career Government Employees and I was not a career employee. To become one, I had to get my name on the career register in Washington D.C. and be rated in the top three on the list. My military time gave me an extra 15 points so I had a good chance of making it to the top of the register. The personnel officers I was dealing with offered me no help. They merely told me that if I could get on the register, they would consider me for the job. Finally, I found one who would help me. He reviewed my application and gave me some hints. Certain words had more impact than others and he helped me finalize the resume. I submitted my paperwork and a few days before I was due to separate from the service I was hired at one of the radar sites as a career employee. We would have to move, but I was going to be a career Government employee. Gerda was thrilled that it had worked out for us. Her dream of job security as fulfilled.

****

Our first three years of civilian life was not easy for Gerda. The system was undergoing major downsizing, and our job was constantly on the line. Gerda's dream of job security was turning out to be a nightmare. We had been in our first location near Birkenfeld, Germany for only a year when we were forced to move. My job was being cut and we needed a job. The depot where I had last worked as a TSgt had an opening and they were happy to hire me. We moved back to the Ramstein area again.

Before that happened some major changes in our life took place. I was working and the boys were in school all day and Gerda was bored. At first she was thrilled that I didn't have to travel in my new job, and that I was home every evening. She had hated that I was gone so much over the last three years. I must admit that I felt the same way. We lived in the middle of nowhere in a tiny little farming town. We had a nice house situated on a small creek, and a nice view. It was a peaceful little town, but there was nothing for Gerda to do.

We bought a new German washing machine and had it installed in the basement utility room. Gerda did a load of wash and while it was working she went upstairs. She heard something and hurried down to the utility room. The washer was walking across the floor and was pulling on the hoses that connected it to the house. She quickly hit the switch and shut it off. When I got home I put it back and we tried it again. When it got to the spin-cycle it started to sway back and forth and move across the room. We shut it off and called the repairman. He came out and of course, the machine worked like a charm. Gerda was ready to do something drastic by this time, but she tried it again. It walked.

She called the factory and in a very firm voice let them know how she felt and told them that she wanted an engineer out there soon. A few days later he arrived, shook the machine and diagnosed the problem. It was a construction error from the factory and they sent us a new washer. This one worked and didn't have the urge to walk around the room.

Another thing happened in the utility room. We discovered that there were mice in the house. Gerda had separated the wash into piles of white, colored, etc., and left them overnight. The next morning when she started to load the washer about half a dozen nice jumped out of the wash and ran around the room. She screamed and beat it up the stairs and went right to a little farm store in the village. She asked for a package of mouse traps. He brought a box out of the back room and she took it. When she got home she found that she had

101

purchased a gross of traps. We had enough traps that we didn't empty them. We simply threw the mouse and trap in the garbage. The first night we set four traps in the laundry room, and by 10p.m. we had caught four mice. We reset the traps and caught several more. Over the next few days we caught more mice. I examined the house and fixed anything where I thought a mouse to could gain access to the house. They were all in the lower floor and we never saw a mouse upstairs where we lived and where the bedrooms were located. The mouse problem was solved.

We had the worst winter the area had seen in about 20 years. There was snow on the ground from November until April and Gerda was trapped in the house alone most of the time.

One evening Gerda turned to me and asked how I felt about getting a poodle to keep her company. I thought it would be ok, but she then asked if I would rather have another baby. We had both privately wished for a little girl, but had never said anything to each other. It seemed that our life was somewhat stable and the idea appealed to me. Within two weeks she was pregnant.

She received her prenatal treatment at the U.S. Army Hospital near where we were living. The pregnancy developed normally and we were making plans for the birth and the changes we would have to make in our life styles and in the house. Then it happened.

Without warning I was told that the workforce was drawing down from twelve positions to three, and mine was included in the reduction. I immediately got on the phone and talked to the Commander of the depot in Ramstein and he had an opening. He had not put it into the system, but he said that he would do it that day and I should apply. I did and he did what he said he would and a few weeks later we were ready to make the move. Gerda was in her ninth month and quite big and now we had to move. It got worse.

We drove down to Ramstein and found a nice house to rent in the town of Rodenbach, only three miles from the base where I would be working. It was a two-story house with all of the bedrooms upstairs. Perfect. Our bedroom would be right next to the new baby's room so Gerda would be able to hear every little peep the baby would make. She was excited about the move.

We made arrangements for our things to be picked up by the movers, and I went to my new job. I was told that I should immediately report to Site Wasserkuppe because they needed me there. I complained to civilian personnel and was told that there was nothing I could do. Either report to Wasserkuppe or resign my position. I went home and told Gerda what was happening and that I had to go. She was not happy and told me so. This meant that I would be gone and she must prepare for the movers and then contend with them while they packed our stuff and prepared it for the move. What a situation for a pregnant woman in her ninth month, who was quite large and uncomfortable. She did it.

On the day the movers were to come, I left the site at Wasserkuppe and went home without telling anyone that I was leaving. I arrived home and found everything had been sorted by category. Things that shipped, things we needed that night, and arranged so that the packers could, as an example, pack the kitchen items and then when we unpacked we knew exactly where things should go. The entire house was arranged that way. I was speechless.

They packed our things and we moved to Rodenbach where they unloaded everything from the truck. The house was filled with boxes and stuff. As soon as they were gone I left to go back to work and left Gerda with the work of unpacking the boxes etc...

I was gone for about three weeks and returned home and to my new job. Gerda had finished everything she could and the house was almost a home. I don't know how she could do it, but she did. It wasn't too long and Melinda was ready to make her appearance. Gerda went into labor in the middle of the day. I took her to Landstuhl Army Hospital, and they examined her and told her she was not dilated enough and to go home and come back later when the contractions were closer. They were already happening about every five minutes but we did what we were told.

About two hours later I couldn't stand to see her in such pain, and I took her back to the hospital. This time they kept her. Soon after that her water broke and it was filled with blood. They wanted to contact me, but we did not have a phone and I was home with the boys. They told her that the life of the baby was in danger. Several doctors were called and they worked to save the baby and Gerda. When I called the hospital from a pay phone Melinda had been born and the crisis was past. That was not the end of the saga.

I visited Gerda that day and met my new daughter. They were both beautiful. The next morning, I woke up with a fever of 102f. There was no way I could go to the hospital with a fever and sore throat. I called in sick and stayed home. They had told me at the hospital that she would be in the hospital for three days, so I was planning on picking them up on the appointed day. They released her a day early. Gerda was packed and had her baby in her arms, but there was no one to pick her up. She felt like an abandoned child with nowhere to go and no one to help her. She finally called my work place and they sent someone to the house to tell me to get up to the hospital and pick up my family. I raced to the hospital and brought them home. Gerda was not happy with me.

It was thrilling to have our baby daughter home with us. That first night somewhere around midnight the baby cried. Gerda go up and fed her and changed her diapers. She laid her back in her little bed and turned off the lights. Gerda was suddenly struck with the magnitude of our decision. In one room was a tiny baby totally dependent on us, and in the next room were two more children who were equally dependent on us for their life, safety and welfare. The emotion was almost overwhelming as she stood there in the dark. *My God what have we done?*

Within a few days Gerda settled into being the mother of an infant. This time she had a washing machine and dryer so laundry chores were greatly simplified. No more cooking the wash on the kitchen stove and bending over the bathtub to rinse. It didn't take long until she started getting bored and look for some way to fill the time. One of the men I worked with at my last site had also moved to the Ramstein area. His wife Nell was taking oil painting lessons and invited Gerda to join her. We bought tubes of paint, brushes, paint thinner and some blank canvases. She was ready to become the next Monet.

The lady next door loved Melinda and wanted to babysit her whenever possible. Twice a week Nell and Gerda went to lessons. They dropped Melinda off at the neighbor's house and went to the studio. Both of them were quite good and Gerda learned fast. She had a new hobby which she really enjoyed doing. She never became an artist who could create a picture in her mind and then transfer it to canvas, but she could copy from a photo or other pictures. Her paintings are hanging in many homes around the world. She didn't sell any, she just gave them away. She never liked her finished paintings, so she wouldn't take money for something she didn't like.

A year after moving to Ramstein I had an opportunity for a promotion to GS-11, but I would have to move again. I took the promotion and we moved to site Wasserkuppe on the East German border, near the town of Fulda. We found a nice home being built in a little town of Ried near the foot of the mountain. There was only one problem; it would be a month before it would be finished and we could move in. We found a nice hotel in a neighboring village and rented two rooms for a month. I went to work; the boys went to school and Gerda sat in a hotel room with Melinda. That is when she learned to play solitaire.

We ate all of our meals in the hotel restaurant. After a month, Gerda was sick of restaurant food and couldn't wait to get her own kitchen and cook our meals. We moved into our new home. It was big and beautiful, but it wasn't quite finished. The landlord came every weekend and worked on the areas that needed finishing. Very soon our lives were back to normal.

Gerda continued to paint whenever Melinda was taking a nap or in her play pen. One day she had been painting and had a pallet full of paint. We finally had a telephone and it rang. Melinda was awake and playing. While Gerda was talking, Melinda found her paint filled pallet and proceeded to paint herself and anything else she could reach. It took hours to clean up the mess. Gerda put the paints away and never painted again. Sad, because she had become very good.

While I was still in the Air Force and we were living in Kindsbach, each summer we would spend two weeks on vacation in Denmark on the North Sea. It was a time when I was totally free of stress from work and Gerda was free of the boredom of staying at home. The boys bought kites and flew them a lot. We ate food we had never had before; I drank great Danish beer and the boys drank endless bottles of bright colored soft drinks. Every day we went to a Danish bakery and picked up pastries of all kinds. Rain or shine we took long walks on the beach and just relaxed and had fun.

This year would be Melinda's first time at the beach. She had just learned to walk and at home in Ried we had steps front and back, so she could not just come and go as she liked. The cabin we rented was at ground level and she ran in and out of the house all day long. At the beach, she immediately took off her pants and sat bare bottomed in the sand. You could put them on and in two minutes she had them off again. It didn't matter because the beach was "clothing optional".

Every day at noon the boys walked to a little restaurant and ate fish and chips for lunch. We gave them each ten Kroner and off they went. Melinda took a nap and then it was off to the beach for some fun in the sand. Gerda was always very relaxed during our vacations and she looked forward to them each year.

Not long after we arrived at Site Wasserkuppe civilian personnel discovered that they had made a mistake in letting me take the promotion, and informed us that we needed to return to the United States because we had been overseas for six years. The official policy at that time was that you could spend five years overseas and then you must be assigned in the states for at least two years before you were eligible for another overseas assignment. The Air Force had a central referral system in which you could enroll and if you were picked for an assignment you had to take it, no matter where it was, or resign your appointment. We were selected for assignment to a radar site in the town of North Truro, MA. Right near the tip end of Cape Cod. It was time for Gerda to organize another move, her fourth in three years.

CHAPTER FOURTEEN

CAPE COD TO CALIFORNIA
SEPTEMBER 1972 TO FEBRUARY 1975

When a family packs up and moves to another country, it is no small thing. There are many decisions that must be made and many of the actions are dependent upon the completion of other actions. To do it successfully and with a minimum of disruption it takes a plan.

There are two types of shipments; household goods and hold baggage. The household goods are the furniture and items that will be packed and shipped by boat and take about three months to arrive at the next destination. The hold baggage is items you need right away. Extra clothes, some kitchen item, or things needed to set up housekeeping until the household goods arrive. They are shipped by air and are usually available within a few days of arriving.

Since I was working, all of the planning, shorting and arranging of the items to be shipped fell to Gerda. She was a master at organizing everything, and our moves always went smoothly because of it.

When we left Germany the first time, Elisabeth was healthy and able, now she was handicapped by the paralysis on her left side, and spent her days sitting on the sofa looking out a small window and working crossword puzzles. We had been helping her parents whenever we could, doing anything that needed to be done. Now we were leaving. Who would help when they needed something? Who would take care of all the little things that we did? Gerda was very concerned, but she also knew that there was no choice and life was not always the way we wanted it to be. We packed up and moved to Cape Cod, USA.

Surprise! When I reported in we were told that the site was being phased out and would be closing in four months. The site would be kept functioning in caretaker status, and would be used by the engineers from Boston. There would be a Reduction-in-Force or RIF and all but three civilians would be let go. I was the senior civilian on site so I would not lose my job, but we were suddenly faced with the prospect of causing a native of Cape Cod to lose his job. I got on the phone and soon located a position in Riverside, California. Our move would be extended to California. It would take four months for all of the approvals to go through so we had to find a way of surviving until we could move on.

We rented a summer cabin in Harwich, MA and set up housekeeping with the hold baggage we had shipped. Gerda had made an outstanding choice in selecting what we would need, and we were able to get by very well. We registered the boys in school and I went to work. Gerda was left with Melinda and there was no one in the neighborhood she knew.

Gerda decided that she would like to learn to sew thinking that she would be able to sew many of Melinda's things. She enrolled in an evening course so that I could drive her to and from the lessons. The very first class she met a very nice woman who was a descendent of the captain of the Mayflower from 1620 fame. She offered to pick Gerda up and provide transportation when she needed something. They became good friends and enjoyed their time together.

The beaches on Cape Cod are wonderful and after Labor Day almost empty. During the summer months, the place is packed with tourists resulting in traffic jams and confusion. Labor Day summer ends and the crowds are gone. We arrived on the day following Labor Day and thus we missed the crowds. We went to the beach often in the late summer evenings and on the weekends. We were getting accustomed to the life on the Cape when it was time to leave.

Our household shipment had arrived and the Air Force agreed to forward it on to California. We kept the things we had shipped hold baggage and loaded everything in the car for the trip west. It was late December when we left and snowing. We had not been home to see my parents for six years and we were anxious to go to Mount Vernon and see them. We would be spending Christmas with them, so we had to take all of the Christmas presents for the kids with us in the car. I don't know how I managed to get everything in the car, but I did. Hold baggage, Christmas presents, three kids and two adults, all loaded in Plymouth Fury III. It was a big car but it was fully loaded.

Gerda set up her deli in the back seat and we left. She rode in the back seat for the entire trip west. Melinda sat in a small primitive car seat in the middle position. Ron and Gerald took turns sitting in the front with me and sitting next to Melinda. They changed places every couple of hours. The first night was spent in Niagara Falls, NY. We got up early and had breakfast in the motel restaurant. It had snowed about eight inches during the night so I called the highway patrol office and asked if the highway was open. They told me there were no problems. Wrong answer.

The lake affect snow was blowing in off Lake Erie and we were soon in whiteout conditions. Around ten in the morning Gerda saw a motel sign and we pulled in and got a room. The blizzard got worse and by evening the highway was closed and the National Guard was called out to use their tracked vehicles to rescue folks who were stranded along the highway. The motel soon filled up and the conference rooms and halls were filled with beds. The National Guard provided folding cots and sleeping bags for the stranded folks. That's how we lived for the next day and night. No one could come or go.

Gerda was impressed with how everyone conducted themselves. Complete strangers stepped in and helped wherever they could. Cooks, waiters, bar tenders and anything else that was needed, all without pay. When the bar ran out of beer no one complained. It was quite an experience. The next day the storm passed and we headed west once again.

We were shocked by how my parents had aged in the past six years. We both vowed to never stay away that long again. In spite of the shock, we had a perfect Christmas with Mom and Dad, and enjoyed it very much.

We headed south for California, but we stopped in Long Beach, WA to see my sister Vivian and her family. The day we were to leave Long Beach, Gerda awoke with a sore throat and a fever of 103°F. We went to the doctor who gave her some antibiotics and cough syrup with codeine, and we were off. That night Gerda sat up most of the night because the codeine gave her nightmares. In her dreams, she was running and kept falling in a deep hole and could not get out. Rather than live the horror of the dream she stayed awake as long as possible.

We arrived in Riverside, CA and found a house to rent. We leased it for one year, but it was not yet empty and it would be a couple of weeks before it was ready. We had to get the kids into a school and I had to work, so we found an old motel where the school bus would stop and pick up the kids, and we moved in. It was not very clean, so we went to the store and bought all sorts of cleaning material. Gerda cleaned the place like it had not been cleaned for years. When the landlady came in to talk about a cleaning deposit she took one look inside and said it was ok not to pay a deposit.

We stayed there for two weeks and during that time, a prostitute moved into the next unit and kept us awake all night by turning customers. We told the landlady and she put a stop to that. The next night an old couple moved in much to our delight. Great, old people are always quiet and go to bed early. Wrong answer. By five in the evening they were both drunk and shouted obscenities at each other until after midnight. Gerda was getting to know the seedier underside of American life.

We moved into the house and settled into the California life style. The neighborhood wives, who were not working came and introduced themselves to Gerda and invited her to the neighborhood coffee klatch. The wives and their children who were not in school gathered at one of their houses and talked. Since we were the only one with a big swimming pool our house was the place of choice. At first Gerda liked the company, but soon it became a routine completely void of any meaning. The women talked about their husbands, and their shortfalls. They also talked about their love lives and invited

Gerda to tell about us, but she declined saying that she had nothing to say. In a few weeks Gerda knew, from the other wives, the size and love making capabilities of every man in the neighborhood.

The smog was terrible and all of the kids including Melinda had a constantly runny nose. Family members who visited found it difficult to breathe and complained of a metallic taste in their mouths.

I taught the boys how to swim and almost every evening we gathered by the pool. We sat and watched the boys perform diving events and other water fun. All of us really enjoyed these evenings, and frequently I joined in the fun in the pool. I don't think Gerda every went in the pool. She was afraid of the water and had no desire to go swimming.

Whenever someone came to visit we had to take them to Disneyland which was only a few miles away. I thought it was great fun, but for Melinda it was sheer terror. We only took her once and she was afraid of everything and cried throughout every ride we took her on. Much to the displeasure of the other riders.

We lived in California for two years and life never changed for Gerda. She felt that she was wasting away mentally, and that life had no meaning for most of the women. Several of the women were stoned on valium much of the time. Before Gerda knew this, she wondered how they could stay so calm when the children were driving her crazy.

Melinda was only three and Gerda knew she should stay at home and take care of her until she was in school. Even then she was not sure what she could do. She had learned the German legal system, and knew only how to work in a German environment. She felt trapped in a life style that she could not escape.

And then I got a call from the Commander of the radar Site at Wasserkuppe, Germany. He told me that the site was under contract maintenance and that things were a mess. Would I be willing to come over and straighten things out? I immediately said yes, and in February 1975 we were on our way to Germany.

CHAPTER FIFTEEN
THE MIDDLE YEARS
FEBRUARY 1975 TO JUNE 1995

We found a house in the town of Kuenzell, very near to Fulda, Germany. There was an Army post in Fulda, where they had a commissary, base exchange, and schools. The high school only went through grade 10 necessitating that the older students go to Frankfurt and live in a dormitory. We got the kids enrolled in school and I went to work.

The commander had been right, the maintenance contract was a mess and the site was having way too many equipment failures, and it took too long to be repaired. I had my work cut out for me, but I managed to get a lot of problems solved in just a few months. One great thing about my job was that there was almost no travel involved and no shift work, so every evening I came home, ate dinner and spent the evening with the family.

We had arrived in Fulda in February 1975 and Ron was in the 9th grade. The high school in Fulda only went through ten grades. Ron spent his Sophomore year in Fulda and the following fall he went to Frankfurt and moved into the Dormitory. He would leave every Sunday evening on a military bus and come home the following Friday evening. Gerda hated it. First Ron was her first-born son and the idea that he was living on his own at age 16 was terrifying for her. No 16-year-old should be left alone in a big city with all of its temptations and moral traps. She could imagine numerous scenarios, none of which were to her liking. I don't think a day went by that she didn't say something about how much she hated having Ron living away from home. A year later when he left to attend the University of Washington, it was worse.

In the spring of 1977 I was transferred to Sembach, Germany to work the maintenance contract that was being negotiated for the entire Air Defense System. We moved and found a house in the little town of Schallodenbach, about ten miles from my job and about five miles from the schools at Vogelweh. The family was back together again, at least for a while.

Ronald attended his senior year in Vogelweh High School and graduated in the spring of 1978. He left home that summer and moved to Seattle to attend the University of Washington. The birds were leaving the nest and the reality of life came home to both of us. When we left Ron in Mount Vernon and flew home to Germany Gerda's life was completely upside down. We had taken a few days leave and flown to Mount Vernon and spent some time with the family. Ron found an apartment in Seattle, but it would be three months until school started, and he needed something to do. He stayed with Glen and Irmgard and worked in a cheese factory in Mount Vernon. At the end of the leave, we flew back to Germany.

This is where Gerda's life began to change. Gerald and Melinda were in school all day, and she was alone. During that time alone she thought about Ronald a great deal. The idea that the children were already leaving home and were alone somewhere in a strange city was overwhelming her. She decided she must change her life. But how?

****

She knew that the only way to change her life was to go to work somewhere. All of her legal skills had long since been outdated, and working for a lawyer or the court system was out of the question. She knew nothing about working as an American, and in Germany the only American jobs were U.S. Government jobs. To be hired you had to be an American citizen. And she was not yet a citizen. After days of soul searching and long evenings discussing what to do, Gerda decided that the answer was to apply for a German job on an American facility. As my wife, she already had an identification card which gave her access to the bases and the commissary and base exchanges. She went to the civilian personnel offices of the Air Force Base at Sembach, and to the civilian personnel office in the Army Kaiserslautern Support Area. As part of the applications she was required to take an English Language test. On both tests, she got a perfect score which put her high on the hiring list.

A few weeks later she hit pay dirt. Sembach personnel called and offered her a temporary job working in the Personnel Office. The job was for four months with full pay and benefits. They had gotten behind and a big backload of information had to be entered into the personnel records. She started the job with fear that she could not learn the computer programs she would need to enter the data.

I was working on Sembach Air Base, so we rode together to and from work. The first day when I picked her up she was in tears. "I don't know what I am doing. I have to constantly ask for help and I don't think I can ever learn it." I assured her that it is normal not to know what you are doing on the first day of a new job. The women she was working with told her the same thing and within a week she was loving it.

The job lasted only four months, but by the time it ended she was a changed woman. She had learned the job in just a few days and within two weeks she was working completely on her own. Her attitude changed and her confidence returned. She was not just a helpless housewife with no skills to offer. She could learn any job she could get.

In 1980 Gerald graduated from high school and moved to Seattle to attend the University of Washington. Gerda had struggled with the idea of the kids leaving when Ron left, but by the time Gerald left she had adjusted. I was the one who had difficulty with Gerald's leaving. I missed Ron very much, but when Gerald left, the fact that both boys were gone from home left me feeling old and tired.

In March of 1981 Ludwig suddenly died of a major heart attack. Unknown to us, he had suffered a small heart attack and had not gone to the doctor, or told anyone. When the big one hit, he called the equivalent of 911 and an ambulance soon arrived to pick him up. He had always said that he would never be carried out of his apartment, and that he would either walk out or die inside. By the time the ambulance arrived he had put on a suit and tie and was waiting for them. He walked down two flights of stairs and got in the back of the ambulance and lie down. This automatically told the medical team that he was not very sick and they treated them accordingly. Shortly after arriving at the hospital, he died.

We drove to Wiesbaden and brought Elisabeth to our house where she would live for the foreseeable future. No one had any idea how it would go, and when we could find a care center for her. We thought that we could do it without any problem. How big of a problem could it be to help her to the bathroom and feed her. It should be easy. It didn't happen that way.

The physical aspects of the care were not that difficult. The problem was the mental side of the care. When Elisabeth needed help, or wanted something she didn't speak up. She just looked at Gerda and waited. Sometimes she waited too long to ask to go to the restroom and wet herself trying to get there. Elisabeth did not want to be a burden so she said nothing, which actually made her a bigger burden. Gerda tried to make her understand, but it didn't work. On top of this behavior was a life time of frustration and pain which Gerda carried.

The death of Ludwig and then suddenly having to care for her mother released feelings and resentment in her. She was relieved by the passing of her father. The years of mental and physical abuse she had suffered at his hands came spilling out. Elisabeth became the recipient of Gerda's anger and frustration, not because Gerda blamed her mother, but because she was there. All those years she had never intervened but stood back and let it happen. Gerda was unable to control the emotions that suddenly overwhelmed her and she let them happen.

After one month Bernd located an adult care center in a suburb of Frankfurt. We loaded Elisabeth and her things into the car, and moved her to her new home. She was well taken care of and enjoyed some of the best times of her life while there. The fact that she was happy made the difference. Gerda felt guilty that she had been unable to deal with the situation better, but now her mother was in a place where she was happy and the guilt was gone. Elisabeth remained there for the rest of her life. During her time in the home Gisela visited once a week. With the help of her son, Bernd, she took care of her mother's needs. She bought new clothes when needed. She made sure that her mother's every wish was fulfilled.

****

In August 1981 I flew to Mount Vernon for a family reunion celebrating Mom and Dad's 60th anniversary. I returned to Germany and the next morning my brother Don called to tell me that Dad had suffered a massive stroke and was not expected to live. I flew home and got there just hours before he died. I was able to tell him that I loved him and that it was ok if he let go and passed on. I stayed for the funeral and then returned home. It took me several years to adjust to the death of my father. I was unable to tell the story of his passing without crying. Time is the great healer and I adjusted.

In 1982 Gerda was offered a job as supply clerk at the Department of Defense Junior High School in Sembach. The job had pay and benefits. She monitored all of the special things the teachers needed. This included all of the text books they used in their classes. She also ordered replacement items when the supply on hand got low. The previous person in the position was a young man who had no concept of what he was doing, thus everything was a mess. He had ordered things that he thought the teachers might use or enjoy. They did not need or want most of what he ordered. The supply room was filled with useless things that had wasted thousands of dollars spent for nothing.

Gerda's first task was to inventory and classify everything in the stock room. Determine what the teachers needed and then clear out what was not. Her final task was to determine what the teaching staff required and make sure it was on-hand when they needed it.

Her ability to organize came through and it wasn't long until she had a smooth-running supply system. The person in the same position in the elementary school was a retired Air Force Sergeant who had spent his entire career in supply. Ira Colson knew all of the tricks of the trade, and he was willing to help Gerda in any way he could. I had known Ira for many years. I don't think that influenced him in any way, but he passed on his knowledge to her as fast as she could absorb it. She liked the work because no two days were exactly alike, and she was treated by the majority of the teaching staff as their equal.

Gerda hated it when anyone talked down to her or treated her as if she was below their level in life. That rarely happened in this job.

Her job ended when I was accepted for a position at Wright Patterson Air Base in Dayton Ohio. She had to organize another move, this time an international move. She quit her job and took control of the move and as you would expect had everything organized and prepared when the movers arrived at the door to pack and ship our things.

DAYTON, OHIO
June 1983 to June 1985

We arrived in Dayton on a hot and muggy June day. We moved into the Holliday Inn in Fairborn and I reported to work. I had no time to look for a place to live, so Gerda took over. She called a realtor who was an immense help. They located a house to rent in Beaver Creek, just a few miles from the base.

We talked about buying a place but we knew we did not have the down payment, and when we tried to buy a car, we couldn't get credit. We had lived outside of the United States for so long, we did not have a credit account established and the banks didn't have a clue as to who we were. We finally found someone who would trust us and General Motors (GMAC) financed a new car. We decided to rent for at least a year and then think about buying.

We settled into the mid-western life style. Melinda was 13 and enrolled in middle school. She made friends, some in the neighborhood and some from school. We kept hearing that drugs were a huge problem in Beaver Creek, and that we needed to watch our children very closely. Gerda and one of the neighbor ladies attended a "how to fight drugs" session at the school. It was given by a drug expert from the police force. They explained that you needed to get right in their face if you suspected anything was going on. If a child came home and went right straight to their room, it was a bad sign. Go in and look them in the eye and look for signs of drug use. If signs are there, search their private things looking for pills, or notes or anything out of the ordinary.

Melinda was little bit rebellious and pushed the limits on some things. Gerda took the advice of the police expert and got right in her face. She hated it, because she remembered how her own father had invaded her privacy and how much she disliked it. It had been humiliating to her then, and she did not like what she had to do. She told me that I should leave things to her, it was her daughter and she would handle it. She did.

Gerda bought books about drugs and how to deal with teenagers and lay them on the coffee table. She also read them and took much of the advice to heart. I watched from the sidelines as she took control of every situation, and we all survived a very difficult time.

I was promoted at work shortly after being assigned there. I was a division chief with six women and three men working under me. The work was sometimes interesting, but most of the time it was dull, repetitious and boring. I hated it. I longed for another assignment to Europe, but mostly I wanted to get back to Germany.

Gerda made friends in the neighborhood and was seldom alone during the days. Once again she enjoyed her friends but she was unfulfilled and wanted some way to change her life. I started working everything I knew to find an opening in Germany. It worked and in June 1985 we were headed for Ramstein, Germany to a detachment of the organization at Wright Patterson.

Once again I worked and Gerda organized an international move. By this time, she was getting pretty good at it and it went very smoothly.

RAMSTEIN, GERMANY
July 1985 to June 1995

These were the happiest years of our lives. We were both healthy and young enough to do anything we wanted, and with both of us working we could afford just about anything we wanted. Here is how it all came together.

We arrived in Germany and found a house in a small town of Enkenbach-Alsenborn, a few miles from where I would be working. As soon as we got settled into our new home, Gerda filed for a job with both the Army and Air Force. Again, she had to take an English test, which she passed with no problem.

A few months later the Army offered her a temporary job as a data entry clerk in the Office of Construction Management. They provided contract management and oversight for construction jobs in the Kaiserslautern area. The person who held the job was going on maternity leave for six months and they needed a replacement for her until she returned. Once again Gerda came home in tears. She didn't know anything about contract management and all the terms were strange new words which she had never heard or used. Once again she felt hopeless and knew that she could never learn the terms and jargon of the job.

I had worked in contract management for the Air Force and knew most of the terms that were so confusing to her. I assisted by explaining some of the words and what they meant, and assured her that within a couple of weeks she would know them all. I was right and in a few days, she was an old hand and was regaining her confidence.

The job was not very demanding, and it wasn't long until the job began to be boring. The same thing every day. Different jobs and different companies, but everything else the same. There was a rumor that the girl who owned the job was not going to return from maternity leave, and that it was possible for Gerda to be hired as a permanent employee. She was not sure if she wanted that or not and was torn between do I keep a boring job, or quit and find something more to my liking.

The problem was solved when the girl decided to come back to work and Gerda was released.

One of the circumstances that made her decisions easier was that she worked because she wanted to and not because she had to. If she lost her job it did not affect the family. This was a blessing and a curse. Her ego said that her job was important and that it was vital that she keep working. The reality that I was firmly employed and was meeting the needs of the family, plus a good savings, took the sting out of being released.

Another thing that made it easier was that transportation between Alsenborn and her job was by bus and the schedules required her to change busses. The timing was such that she had to leave early to make the connections. This made for a very long day.

When we got the job in Ramstein, before we ever left the states, we had called a man we knew who had a house which he rented to Americans and asked him if his house in Otterberg was available. It was not. We both knew the Colonel who had rented it, and we were familiar with the house and garden. A few weeks after Gerda left her job with the Army he called and said that the house was available and wanted to talk to us and basically interview us to see if we were acceptable. We were and moved into a home we stayed in for the next nine years.

Within a few weeks Gerda was called by the German personnel office on Sembach Air Base and told that an opening was available in the base transportation system. The office was where all military transportation was arranged. They scheduled all military travel for folks leaving for a new duty station; going on temporary duty; emergency leave; or any other type of travel covered by official military orders. She had no experience in travel, but her English was very good and I was convinced that she could do the job. She was not sure, but she applied and was scheduled for an interview.

She made such a strong impression on the staff conducting the interview that they told her at the end of the session that she had the job. She started the next day. Once again she was frustrated by a new vocabulary of strange terms. She was hired with a six-month probationary period. If at the end of that time her work was satisfactory, she would be hired in a full time permanent position. After several weeks of frustration, she began to understand the requirements of the job and the new jargon of military business. The Air Force thrives on acronyms and both military and civilian travel systems are full of them.

With so much to learn she brought home military regulations and joint travel regulations and studied them. When things in the office were slow, she studied the controlling documents and soon knew the civilian airport codes, the routing codes and the names of all of the Air Force Bases in the U.S. At the end of three months her boss told her that she had passed and that the probationary period was ended. She was hired as a permanent employee. She could not have been more pleased, and I could have not been prouder.

I worked at Ramstein Air Base and she worked at Sembach Air Base. We lived about half way between the two. In the mornings, I went South and she went North. This made it very difficult for me to take her to work and get to my job on time. She spread the word that she needed transportation to work and in a matter of hours Herr Schmidt who lived in the same town we did, called her and offered her a ride. They came to an agreement that she would pay him a certain amount for gas and he would take her to and from work. He also agreed that when he was on vacation or did not go to work, he would arrange for someone else to provide her transportation. The substitute driver was Klaus Vogel. Within a few weeks they were all the best of friends. The arrangement really worked well and Gerda was as happy as I have ever known her to be.

A few months later Gerda was in civilian personnel and noticed a note on the bulletin board explaining that if you didn't feel your job was graded properly you should file for a re-evaluation. Gerda had been moved into the position of office manager and felt that her position should be reclassified. She told her boss that she felt her job was graded too low and she would like to have it looked at. Her boss told her it was being taken care of and she should wait until he notified her. He was lying. He never submitted the request. He had been influenced by one of the other German workers who wanted to be the top dog.

She asked several times about the request and was always told that these things took time. She waited. About nine months later her boss was reassigned and when her new boss arrived she went to him and asked him what the status of her request was. He immediately called personnel and was told that no request had ever been submitted. He was furious and within an hour he had filed the paperwork and told Personnel that he expected results without delay.

Within days the classification specialist from personnel came to the office and watched what Gerda did. After three days, she had seen enough and told Gerda not to worry because things looked favorable. A few days later she received word that her position was being upgraded, not one step but two. This put her in charge of the travel department and on an equal level as the person who had influenced her previous boss. It changed her life.

She had been validated. She was smart enough to do that. She was worthy of the trust people placed in her, and she excelled. Over the next eight years she was selected as employee of the month and employee of the year several times.

I was proud of her and all she was able to do. I had known for years that she could organize and manage complex things, but she had lost her confidence. It was back and it was nice to see.

Away from work we loved living in the house at number 10 Alleestrasse in Otterberg, Germany.

****

On July 21, 1986, I turned 50. We had a party. What a party it was. It started on Friday and ended late Sunday evening. We invited all of our German family and friends. Eighteen in all. They gathered with tents and camping trailers and parked them in our orchard. We had a half acre orchard with two cherry trees, two Italian Plum trees and five apple trees, with a lot of space in between for camping. We also had a good-sized swimming pool with a large pergola overlooking the pool. It was quite a party.

Gerda planned the menu and insisted that we serve only American food. We did allow German beer to be served. Several kegs in fact, but we won't go there. Over the weekend we served corn on the cob, hamburgers and cheese burgers, baked potatoes; porterhouse steaks; shrimp cocktails, with all the condiments.

Mornings we served an American breakfast with sausage, beacon, and scrambled eggs. Gerda did all of the prep work and most of the cooking. I worked the BBQ and our nephew Bernd helped in the kitchen. We had so much fun, that we did it again for my 51st and 52nd birthdays.

Bernd and his wife Ingrid went on vacation to Greece and nothing was to their liking so they cut the vacation short and came home. Gerda heard the news and told them to come to our place and use it like a hotel and have a good time. They did. They spent a week with us. We worked and they enjoyed themselves. Most of the time Bernd cooked the evening meal and we loved the company. This set the tone and they visited often during the summer months for the next eight years. To this day, we have a great relationship with Bernd and Ingrid.

In 1989 Gerda's mother Elisabeth died. She had become ill and was moved to a local hospital. We visited her the day before she passed on, and Gerda had the opportunity to tell her she loved her and that it was alright to go. She died quietly in her sleep. After 26 years of being paralyzed from a stroke and sitting, her life came to a quiet end. Gerda was sad but somehow relieved. No more suffering, no more waiting for someone to help you with your normal life's needs, no more being dependent on strangers.

Since the death of Ludwig and her moving to the assisted living home, Elisabeth had enjoyed life in ways many of us might not understand. She learned to manage her wheelchair and was free to move around the facility on her own. Every afternoon she gathered with several of the other women in a social area of the home and visited. Elisabeth became the center of attention and relished the praise and attention she received. Gerda was thrilled that her mother, at last, was receiving the attention she deserved. It made her passing bearable for Gerda and for me.

Also in 1989 the Berlin wall fell and a flood of folks from Eastern Europe moved into what was West Germany. Any German who had lived in Russia under Stalin and had been retained was welcomed to come home, and were given immediate citizenship and a German passport. There were so many of them they overwhelmed the system. Every town in Germany was required to receive a certain number and to provide housing and subsistence for them. Otterberg received a number of Russian families. They didn't fit in the German life style and brought with them some customs that the Germans found to be repulsive. The young folks didn't speak German and found themselves with nothing to do and nowhere to go.

There was a park bench located at the pathway that went past our place where they gathered. They brought beer with them and as the evening progressed they got louder and more of a nuisance. There was a large walnut tree that became their toilet. The bench was under our bedroom window and the noise drove Gerda crazy. She would go out on the balcony and tell them to be quiet. They just laughed and went on with their party.

Every evening Gerda waited for them to arrive. She was obsessed with the Russian and wanted them gone. At least wanted them to take their beer drinking and urinating somewhere else. She went to see the town mayor and he told her that she was not alone and that several folks had complained to him. He also said that there was nothing he could do, but two days later the bench was mysteriously broken up. No one knew how. The next day she came home from work and went to where the broken bench was located and moved the heavy iron legs and base up the hill and hid them in some bushes. I have no idea how she managed to move them because they weighed at least a hundred pounds each. She said that she rolled them end over end but I would swear that she was not strong enough to do it. Her outrage at the Russians must have given her an extra shot of adrenaline that gave her the strength. The Russians never returned to that corner.

In June 1990, my brother Don and his wife Kathleen, my sister Leila and her husband Vic came to Germany for a month visit. We planned their stay so we could see as much as possible in one month. We had an exciting month traveling and eating our way around Europe. During their stay, we decided that the six of us would meet in Calgary Canada and attend the Calgary Stampede. Leila was to make the arrangements.

Shortly after returning home Kathleen had surgery and never left the hospital. Her passing hit me very hard because I had known her since I was a child. I flew home alone and attended the funeral.

In November 1991, my mother died. Gerda decided to stay home so again, I flew alone to Mount Vernon. On the flight, there I wrote an elegy for mom which I read at her funeral.

In July of 1993 Don and his new wife Helen, Leila, Vic, Gerda and I met in Calgary as planned. We flew to Mount Vernon and drove with Don and Helen to Calgary. Leila and Vic met us there at the hotel. It was three days of absolute fun. If you ever get the opportunity to go to the Stampede, go. You will certainly get your money's worth and have an exciting experience.

After returning to Mount Vernon, we had a Herbaugh Family Reunion in Bellingham. Friends and family gathered at the home of my niece Gloria and her husband Ray. It was a beautiful day of renewing relationships with family we had not seen in several years. The entire month visit was one of pleasure and love and we were in no hurry to return to Germany and our jobs.

When we arrived back in Otterberg a strange thing happened to both of us. I walked around the garden and looked at all of the things that I had learned to love and I felt nothing. For the first time in my life I returned to the place I called home and did not feel at home. By the next day I still did not have the feeling of being at home. I brought it up to Gerda and found that she had felt the exact same thing. She was not at home.

I was approaching retirement age from Government service. I had worked for 40 years and had reached my maximum pension. We had been planning what we would do when that time came. For many years, we had planned to retire in Germany and make it our permanent home. We hadn't decided where we would live but we were sure it would be somewhere in Germany.

About a week after returning from vacation we were having our afternoon coffee. We were sitting in the living room looking out our picture window when we both turned towards each other at the same moment and said "I think we should retire in Mount Vernon." We stared at each other for a moment and it was decided. We would retire and move to Mount Vernon and start our new life there where we would be close to family and our children. It was the right decision.

CHAPTER SIXTEEN

RETIREMENT

June 1, 1995 a new and different chapter in our lives began. We both retired. Following a very nice retirement ceremony we left Germany on our way to Mount Vernon, and the rest of our lives.

The retirement was held in the General's Conference center in Headquarters United States Air Forces Europe. I was assigned to the Deputy Chief of Staff for Operations, and the two-star General in charge conducted the ceremony. Both Gerda and I received certificates thanking us for our service, and I was given a letter from President William J. Clinton, thanking me for my years of hard work. I was also given an award and a certificate of retirement. After over 40 years with the Air Force, it was over.

We departed Germany the next day. We flew into Cincinnati, Ohio and then on to Saint Paul, Mi, where we were picked up by Leila who lived in Cumberland Wisconsin. We spent three days with her and her family before we caught a flight for Seattle.

We arrived safely in Mount Vernon, anxious to start looking for a home to buy. Don and Helen invited us to stay with them until we could find a place of our own. Gerda was anxious to see our kids so Don and Helen went camping for the weekend and we held a little family reunion while they were gone. It was a nice way to start retirement.

Prior to coming home, we had written to Dee Donaldson, a real-estate agent, and explained what we were looking for. We called Dee and she had a list of houses that might fit our requirements. The search began. We looked at the places Dee had located but we were not ready to make a decision. One of the places was such a mess outside, with cars and junk piled high, that we didn't even stop and look at it.

We looked at every style of house you can think of and in all of the surrounding towns. Gerda loved several of them but they were out of our price range. We had agreed on how high our mortgage payment could be and still have enough money to live comfortably, and we stuck to the number.

After several weeks of looking, Gerda and her sister Irmgard, went to an open house at the place we had passed because of the junk outside. They called me and told me to get over there because I had to see the place. They were both excited and when I walked in the front door I loved what I saw. The price was right and we made a bid along with some earnest money. We got the place and in mid-July we took possession of our new home.

While the house was empty, we painted, cleaned and put in new carpets. The previous owner had pets and the carpets were a mess. Gerda said that just once she wanted to move into a house without cleaning someone else's food from the stove and refrigerator. We went shopping and put all new appliances in the kitchen and laundry room. We were ready to move into our first house that was truly our home.

Our household goods shipment from Germany arrived on July 31st. We were pleased to see that there was no damage to any of the furniture pieces and none of our glass ware was broken. It was a perfect move.

Just a few weeks into retirement, Don asked if we would like to join Kiwanis. His son Roger was a member and he told Don that they were organizing a new club and were looking for potential members. We didn't know what Kiwanis was so we did some research. They are a community service organization whose primary focus is children. We both liked what we saw and we started attending the meetings.

We met every Tuesday at the Mount Vernon Senior Center. Within a few weeks there was enough of us attending the meetings to allow us to become an official Kiwanis Club, and receive our charter from Kiwanis International. I was elected the Charter President, Helen became Charter Secretary, and Don and Gerda served on the Board of Directors.

Through the Kiwanis Club we discovered many ways to volunteer and to become a part of the local community. While living in Germany, we had never been intergraded into the local society. No matter how good my German was, or how many local business folks I knew, I was always *"that American who speaks good German."* Gerda was always known as my wife.

We immersed ourselves in community activities. Once a week we delivered Meals-on-Wheels to around thirty people. I drove the car and Gerda delivered the meals to the door. It was very fulfilling for her because for many of the recipients she was the only person they saw that day. The route we served took about two hours of our time, but we both enjoyed it. We did that every Wednesday for five years.

I served as a docent in an art museum for eight years. Together we volunteered at an Alternative High School, we participated in many Kiwanis projects. We both became known in Mount Vernon, and suddenly Gerda was no longer known only as *Mrs. Herbaugh*, she was *Gerda.* A woman standing alone on her own merits. It was a time which we both enjoyed very much.

Soon after moving to Mount Vernon, we joined Avon United Methodist Church. Not because we were Methodists, but because we really liked the pastor. The church was also located in the neighborhood where Don and I had grown up. We found that we knew many of the older folks who attended. It was very good to meet people we had known when we were kids. Don, Helen, Gerda and I attended Avon for many years and loved the fellowship we had. We invited Irmgard to join us and she did. For several years, Gerda, Irmgard and I took an active role in the life of the church. We joined a bible study group and for ten years we studied the bible, precept by precept.

In July 1999, my cousins in Nebraska organized a Herbaugh Family Reunion, to be held in Hemingford, NE. Gerda and I drove back to attend. It was nice to see cousins I had not seen in over 40 years. The day of the reunion everyone gathered at the family home. It was a hot July day with the temperature holding around 103 degrees. I drank a lot of water and stayed in the shade as much as possible. Some of the guys drank beer all day and it didn't seem to bother them. They were from Nebraska so they were acclimated to the summer heat.

The following day Gerda and I headed East to Wisconsin to visit Leila and her family.

This was the start of our road trips. Each year in September when school had started and the tourists had thinned to only the old retired folks, we hit the road. For the next ten years, we traveled around the Western United States, and loved every minute of it.

We visited national park after national park, and between the parks we stopped at everything that sounded interesting. Overall, the first fifteen years of retirement were some of the best years of our lives. We had enough money to spend, and plenty of time to do whatever gave us pleasure.

In 2009 I decided to write a book in which I told stories from my life. I had a lot of fun writing it and Gerda and I spent hours discussing what happened when. I published it in 2011.

During the past few years our lives have slowed down and we have dropped out of most of our volunteer positions. I write some every day, and Gerda reads. If she is not doing something else she is reading. I don't have a clue how many books she has read, but it is a lot. At least one per week.

The Kiwanis club where we were charter members closed. Most of the members were senior citizens and many of them got too old to do the things the club required. They didn't want to be part of a club if they could not take part in the service projects. We voted to close the club and Gerda resigned from Kiwanis. I transferred my membership to another club in Mount Vernon, but since then I have also resigned. It was once fun, but neither of us miss it at all.

We also left Avon Church and started going to a big church in Mount Vernon. It is one of those where you can attend for two years and the pastor will not know who you are. It is just too big. Gerda likes to disappear into the crowd, but I like to be in the middle of things doing hands-on stuff.

It no longer matters because as you will see in the next chapter everything changed.

CHAPTER SEVENTEEN

AML

It was a beautiful late summer day near the end of September 2015 when the sky fell in on our heads. Gerda, had been treating her type two diabetes for several years, but she had never taken it as seriously as I had wished. She had some blood drawn a few days earlier and was expecting a high A1C reading. When the phone rang, I could see that it was her doctor calling, so I asked her to take the call. I listened in on the extension phone.

"Gerda, this is Doctor Creelman. I have the results of your blood test and I need to talk to you about it. Can you come in the office tomorrow at 2 pm?"

"Yes, I think I can come. Why? Is there something wrong?" She wanted to know.

"Yes," he replied "but I don't want to talk about it over the phone. I will see you tomorrow.

She turned to me and said that her A1C must really be high for him to want to see me right away.

I agreed. "All we can do is speculate, so there is no reason to worry about it now. We will know soon enough."

As soon as we arrived Gerda was taken to an examination room where she met with Sandra, the PA who had been treating her diabetes. The doctor came to the waiting room and asked me to come with him. We went to the treatment room where Gerda and Sandra were waiting. He never mentioned her A1C, but went right to the results of her annual CBC or blood evaluation.

"Your red cells are ok, but your white cells are way too high and your platelet count is very low. You have only 73 when normal is between 150 and 400. There is something going on in your body that we have to find immediately. Take this slip to the lab next door and they will expedite the results. I will call you tomorrow when I get them."

"This must be serious if you need results so fast." I stated.

"Yes it can be very serious. It could be cancer, but let's wait for the results of this test. I will call you as soon as I know something."

We left his office with a sinking feeling in the pit of our stomachs. The lab is right next to the doctor's office so we went there first. They drew blood and told us they would expedite the results.

Driving home Gerda was silent and I was scared half to death. *If the doctor is so worried and wants test results right now, it must be bad. The only thing I can think of that is related to blood is leukemia. Dear God, it can't be that.* I thought. I didn't say anything because I knew Gerda must be scared enough without bringing up the idea of Leukemia.

We were only home for an hour when the phone rang. It was Doctor Creelman. I answered.

"The pathologist from the lab in Seattle called me and he is very concerned. It looks like Gerda has leukemia and it is fast moving. I called the Cancer Care Center in the Skagit Valley hospital and talked to the doctor on duty. You have an appointment at ten am tomorrow. Can you make it?"

"What kind of leukemia are you talking about?" I asked.

"Let's let the oncologist make that determination, but it is not good news when the pathologist calls with the test results." He assured me.

"Thanks Paul, I'll stay in touch."

I hung up the phone and told Gerda what the doctor had said. She turned pale but didn't say anything. Neither of us slept well that night.

We met Doctor Kojouri. the next morning at ten. We both immediately liked him. We talked about her past medical history and the symptoms that lead up to the blood tests. One of the things he wanted to know was did she ever have something called *Myelodysplastic Syndrome* (MDS). Neither of us had ever heard of MDS so he explained that it was a blood disorder that damaged the bone marrow and inhibited the production of new blood cells. It sometimes led to *Acute Myeloid Leukemia* (AML). After discussing the blood results, he told us that he needed to do a bone marrow biopsy, and that he had time to do it right then. Gerda had heard stories of how painful the test was and was a little hesitant to do it. Doc. Kojouri explained that he could not get an exact diagnosis without it, and she said yes.

Doc. Kojouri was skilled and the biopsy was almost painless. He had distracted Gerda from the exam and she focused on his words and not on what he was doing. He told her that he would have the results in about three days.

I sent a text message to Ron, Gerald and Melinda, asking them to call me when they could. I said that it was important so please call as soon as possible. Each one called within an hour and we explained what was going on. Each one took the news in their own way. I told them that I would contact them as soon as we received the final diagnosis.

Three days later, we were in Doctor Kojouri's office waiting for the results. His face was very solemn when he came into the room and we both knew the news was not going to be good. He got right to the results. Yes, she had MDS and it had progressed into AML. He explained that there was treatment for both diseases, but that the survival rate was very poor when someone had both, especially in older people. (that is anyone over 60) He also explained that the treatment would not cure the AML but could extent her life for an unknown period.

I asked him what that meant in real time. He told us that if we did nothing she would die within a few weeks. If the treatment worked it could extend her life for about four months, but maybe a little longer.

The first type of treatment option was radical chemotherapy which would attack the cancer cells directly, but it would require a month in the hospital, and the probability that she could not survive the treatment was very high.

The second option was a series of injections of a drug called Vidaza, which entered the DNA of the cancer and switched off the gene that directed the cells to multiply. The drug was approved for treating MDS but was not yet approved for AML.

I called the kids and gave them the results of the biopsy and the proposed treatments.

I went online and researched everything I could find on the disease and the proposed treatments. The three kids did the same, and we all came to the same conclusion. Go with the Vidaza. She would receive injections every day for seven days, and then have 21 days to recover and then repeat the cycle.

Gerda started the injections the following day. The list of side effects is long and scary, but she tolerated it very well.

On the day of her first injection we checked in at the front desk and were directed to the lab for a blood draw. Everything is right in one area so no walking around looking for something. In about 30 minutes a nurse called Gerda's name and asked us to come with her. I was asked to come too, because everyone needs moral support the first day. We were taken to a long room with windows all around making it light and open. Along the side of the room were 16 reclining chairs for the patients and other chairs for the visitors.

The nurses were like angels in human form. They were gentle and caring and we both immediately felt like they truly cared about her as a person and not just as a patient. I cannot stress enough how important it is that you like and feel comfortable with the doctor and the nurses. Gerda was very anxious about what was going to happen to her. April, was the name of the first nurse who treated her. April made her feel comfortable and talked her through the injection procedure. *This is going to be tolerable*, we both thought.

Five days into the first treatment series she came down with double pneumonia and was hospitalized. The next day the hospital doctor told me that Gerda would not make it through the day and would go into respiratory collapse and die by evening. I called Betsy and Gerald and asked Betsy if she would call Ron and Melinda. They all rushed to the hospital and waited. Over the next three days we waited and Gerda hung on. She has no memory of those first five days in the hospital, and that is just as well. It was a struggle to keep her alive, but I believe that God had a hand in her recovery.

A few days after the diagnosis our primary care doctor, Dr. Creelman went on vacation to Texas. While he was there he called me every day to see how things were progressing with Gerda and if there was anything he could do to help. We were both impressed with the level of caring he showed for Gerda.

I had called Fordell and others I knew who believed in the power of prayer. They all prayed. I have no idea how many are still praying for her recovery, but it is a host of folks.

After eleven days, she came home. She was on oxygen for two weeks, and had a visiting nurse and physical therapist come in several times a week, for a month. I cooked, cleaned house and did all of the things around the house. Together we made shopping lists and I did the shopping. She rapidly regained her strength and interest in life. At the end of the month Gerda was doing many of the things she had always done. She took over the cooking and much of the housekeeping chores. The fantastic thing is that she had very few side effects from the injections. Life was almost normal, but not entirely. Her platelet count was low so she bruised easily. Her Hemoglobin was low so she was anemic and needed transfusions.

Her immune system was almost totally destroyed by the AML and the injections, so we had to be very careful not to expose her to any outside illnesses.

In November, she completed her second round of Vidaza, and again had few side effects from the treatment. We usually celebrate Thanksgiving at Gerald and Betsy's place, along with the other kids. We asked the doctor and he said it would be fine to go, but if anyone had any symptoms of a cold or flu, to stay away from that person. He advised Gerda to wear a mask, but it is hard to eat Thanksgiving dinner with a mask on, so she ignored the advice most of the day.

Over the next few months Gerda received platelet transfusions, and blood transfusions and continued her monthly infusions of Vidaza.

December arrived and she again took the Vidaza injections. She needed several blood transfusions, but otherwise she was almost normal. She did most of the things she had always done, and I filled in helping with the things she could not do. Christmas was fast approaching, and we brought the tree in from the garage and put it in the living room. We unpacked all of the Advent and Christmas items and Gerda decorated the tree. I took her picture and then went into the bathroom and cried. All I could think of was that *this was going to be our last Christmas together.*

Together, Gerda and I made cookies and prepared for the holidays. The family was here for Christmas Eve, and Melinda and Sophia stayed for Christmas day. Gerda was able to prepare the typical Christmas food. We had a special time sharing our love for each other. Somehow Gerda's illness has rekindled our deep and abiding love for each other, and for the children. It is the silver lining of a very dark cloud.

****

January 16, 2016: Some days are great, but some day's suck. Today Gerda is having a bad day. She got a platelet transfusion yesterday, and to keep from breaking out in hives, she takes Benadryl. This makes her so sleepy that she feels like she is in slow motion. This morning she wanted to make some vegetable soup and was cutting the veggies. Suddenly she became nauseous and week. Broke out in a cold sweat and just felt terrible. In a few minutes, it passed and she lay down and was soon sleeping.

When she has a bad day, I have a bad day, but I can't show it. It turns my stomach and I want to cry, but I smile, take her temperature and blood pressure, and give her encouragement. I can't talk to the kids about it because they are just as affected by everything as I am, so I just smile when I don't feel like smiling, I comfort when I need comforting myself. I pray when I think that God has forgotten about us but I don't hear an answer. Maybe He does answer, maybe He is healing her and I just can't tell yet. Maybe we will have many more years together. That is what I pray for, and that is what I live for right now, but when Gerda has a bad day, doubt rushes in and I don't know what to do about it.

****

February 15, 2016: The platelet count was the first to return to normal, followed a month later by her red count and HGB levels. She was no longer anemic. This ended the need for transfusions and restored a great deal of her energy and ability to function much the way she always had. Our life was almost normal again except for her immune system. It remained very low necessitating caution in her interface with other people and causing us to avoid crowds.

We are also very careful about what she eats. Anything that will be eaten raw must be washed and then sanitized in a mild Clorox solution, and washed again. This includes fruits and vegetables. The kitchen cabinets are washed down and sanitized with wipes every day. And then we go through hand soap and hand sanitizer by the bottle. When we bring the groceries home from the store and finish unpacking them, we sanitize the cabinets again and wash our hands. It may be overkill, but it seems to be working. At first it seemed like a lot of work and too much bother, but now it is the normal way to function and we do it without thinking.

During the time, she was receiving blood transfusions iron began to build up in her liver. This is a normal occurrence and was expected to happen. Her Ferritin count was elevated and we were told that when it reached 1000 she would be put on a medication to remove the iron and that her body had no means to do so on its own. The medication had a list of side effects that would scare you half to death, including loss of vision. I was very worried about her taking it. Her ferritin count rose to 927 and the doctor said that if it continued to rise she must start the medication. Her need for transfusions stopped and her ferritin count dropped on its own to 748. We were all thrilled. It has continued to drop and on May 2, 2016, it was 686. The doctor doesn't know how her body is processing the iron but it is and that is what counts. As long as she doesn't need further transfusions she should be good. We both believe it is an answer to prayer.

As we go forward we don't know how long the Vidaza will hold the leukemia in remission, but we hope and pray for complete remission. We live one day at a time. Gerda has handled her illness very well. She knows that with or without illness we are within a few years of dying, so the fact of dying is not a problem, it is how will she die. Together we hold hands and face the unknown.

****

June 3, 2016: Saw Dr. Kojouri today and he explained that he was very happy with Gerda's recovery and that the prognosis had improved. She is in the middle of her ninth series of Vidaza injections and is scheduled for her 10th series to start on June 23rd. Most of her blood readings have returned to normal, and her immune system has recovered a little bit. Dr. Kojouri informed us that following her 12th series he would do another bone marrow biopsy, and see exactly what condition the cancer is in. We pray that it is in total remission, but we will continue to take life one day at a time.

During the past nine months, we have both thought a lot about death and dying. When it is staring you right in the face it is hard to ignore. We both feel that our spiritual life is in order and that if heaven exists we will be welcomed home. We both know that under all circumstances we are only a few years away from the inevitable, so that is not the issue. Who will be left behind is a worry. A few months ago, it appeared that I would be the one, and that I would have to learn to live without her. Now we don't know, but whoever it is, it will be tough to make the adjustment. We have spent over fifty-six years together and for the last twenty-two years we have been together twenty-four hours a day, seven days a week. But each of us must die alone. It is frightening to think that one of the most important things in your life must be done alone, without the partner you love and trust above all else. We are connected in ways that young people find difficult to understand. Whatever happens it will be difficult to cope with, but what choice do we have? Hang on, pray, and enjoy the time we have together to the utmost.

****

June 23, 2016: Gerda started her 10th series of injections. She had blood work done and we got the results the next day from Dr. Kojouri. Many of the readings were normal and he explained that he was not worried about the other ones. He explained each one again, and why he was not concerned. He then scheduled her for the 11th series.

Each time she starts a seven-day series of injections she has some side effects. For the first two days, her teeth hurt, the injection sites itch and are painful. We found a cortisone cream that really helps so she applies that liberally to the sites every evening. She takes an anti-nausea medication before each injection, and it causes her to be constipated, really constipated. After some experimentation, she found that a morning dose of Mira-lax helps everything move. It is still, never the less, painful. For the next five days, she is able to function pretty well, but the whole process beats her down, both physically and mentally. The week following the chemo, she recovers and then for the next two weeks we live life as normally as we can. We continue to pray for full remission at the end of the year. Maybe, just maybe the good Lord with grant that to us.

****

July 1, 2016: The 10th series has been the most difficult for Gerda. Today she received the last shot in the series. She was emotionally very fragile and could cry about anything. She complained that she was cold, and I offered to get her a warm blanket. She said no thanks, and started to cry. At times like this we are both completely helpless. She doesn't know why she is crying and I don't know what to do to comfort her. In a few moments, it passed and she was smiling again. Later in the evening we were eating homemade tacos when she suddenly started to cry and apologized that she could not help me clean the kitchen and wash the dishes. She just didn't have the strength to do it. I held her for a moment and assured her that it was ok.

Gerda is struggling to keep her blood glucose levels in check. It is cherry season and Washington cherries are the best in the world. She loves cherries. She loves all fruit, but cherries are her favorite. This is when reality catches up with both of us. We both know that this could be the last cherry season we will see together, and so what if her blood sugar is a little high for a few days. Gerda decided that she was going to enjoy her cherries and the rest be damned. I find no argument that would support doing otherwise, so I buy cherries and we sit together and eat them.

****

July 14, 2016: I will turn 80 on July 21, 2016 and Gerda is planning a family party on the following Saturday. I just want a family picnic with hamburgers and wieners, with some good potato salad. That is what she is going to do, but she wants this to be the best birthday I have ever had and she wants to give it to me as a present. She knows that I will never be 80 again, and that this might be our last birthday together. I didn't mean to put her under so much stress, but I know she wants to do it, and it will be a fun day. It will be great to have the entire family together again.

I have been having some problems with my heart. The rhythm is a little off, and when I monitor my pulse it feels like it skips a beat. The doctor explained that it is not life threatening, and I should not worry about it. I worry about it anyway. The problem is that Gerda worries more than I do and that puts her under additional stress. I have also been having a lot of pain in my left knee, which causes her to worry more about me. She doesn't need more stress, and it does not help her healing process. That causes me to worry about her which doesn't help my healing processes, thus the endless cycle goes on, around and around.

****

August 1, 2016: The pain in my knee stopped on its own and feels fine now. We were both relieved.

My birthday came and went and we both had a wonderful time. The family gathered and we spent the day celebrating. It was a fantastic love filled day. It was special for both of us. There were 15 of us and we ate a lot of hamburgers and wieners. Gerda made a great potato salad and tried a new recipe for pasta salad. Both were delicious and I ate more than I should have. Ron, Melinda and Gerald all helped out with the cooking, set-up and serving. I was full to the point of being uncomfortable by the end of the day. It could not have been a better day. It was perfect.

My heart rhythm still bothers me and that upsets Gerda. I wore a Holter Monitor for 48 hours and the results were declared to be normal. I have an appointment with a cardiologist on Aug 15th and we will discuss the meaning of "normal".

We saw Dr. Kojouri on August 2nd and he explained how he expects the future to play out for Gerda. She will complete the 12th series of chemo the end of August and is scheduled to have a bone morrow biopsy on September 13th. The results of the biopsy will not change the treatment with Vidaza, and she will continue each month just as she has been. It will give us a better prognosis and understanding of how the cancer is reacting and help us to project how long her life can be extended.

We both have mixed feeling about knowing how long. The way it is now we just live from day-to-day and blindly accept that it could go on forever. We know it will not and that it will end one day, but do we really want to know when? We must decide by the middle of September so we can advise the doctor about how much to tell us. I hate to make this kind of decision, because I am having difficulty accepting that my life's partner will soon leave me and I will be alone with no one to share the joy of the flowers and sunsets and all the little things we have shared for over 50 years. It is terrifying. Do I really want to know how much time we have?

This summer the flowers have been very beautiful. Everything has bloomed in profusion providing the yard and garden with a flood of color and beauty. I am enjoying it, but I can't escape the feeling that this is God's way of telling us that it will be Gerda's last summer and he is making it extra nice for her. We should share the pleasure it brings.

****

Aug 15, 2016: I saw the cardiologist today and was pleased with the visit. He spent a lot of time with me and listened very carefully. He assured me that there was a cause for my irregular heart beat and he would do his best to find it. He also assured me that it is not life threatening and that there is no reason for me to worry. The Holder Monitor results show that it is too soon to give me a pace-maker, but that I will probably need one someday.

Gerda was very relieved that the cardiologist was working with me to find the cause and develop a treatment plan. It took a huge burden off her shoulders.

****

August 30, 2016: Gerda finished the 12th cycle of Vidaza injections. During the past several series of injections, by the end of the series she was very fragile emotionally and was often upset by little things and cried more than usual. This time she was not. In fact, she seemed to have more energy than ever before. We hope it is a sign that the illness is losing its grip on her and she is getting better. On Friday, the 26th we saw Dr. Kojouri but he did not schedule the next Vidaza injections. We don't know what that means, but we will find out after the biopsy.

****

September 13, 2016: The bone marrow biopsy was done today and it was not as easy as the first one a year ago. Gerda had time to think about what was going to happen, and then when she was called back for the procedure there was a new nurse assisting the doctor. She was in training and everything had to be explained to her, step by step. All of this made Gerda very upset and she had to be given a tranquilizer to calm her.

She was tired for the rest of the day. We will find the results of the biopsy on Tuesday, Sept 20th. They also scheduled the 13th round of Vidaza starting on Monday Sept 19th. It appears as if this will be how we spend the rest of her life. We continue to pray for healing, but that might not be the answer we receive. No is also an answer.

Lyle E. Herbaugh

****

September 20, 2016: Yesterday Gerda started her 13th series of Vidaza and had some lab work done. Today we saw Doctor Kojouri and received the news. First the blood work was not good. Her immune system was so low it was non-existent. The desired number for her ANC count (Absolute Neutrophils Count) is 1000. Gerda had a reading of 72. On top of the immune system, the marrow contained 11% cancer. The doctor expected a count of somewhere between 2.6 and 22, so 11 is right in the middle. It means that the cancer is not multiplying and gives some hope that the treatments will continue to be effective.

To treat the low ANC, she will start taking a new medicine on October 4th. It is called Neuprogen and is designed to increase the white cell count and build up the immune system. We hope and pray that it works.

Each Vidaza series seems to get a little more difficult for Gerda. By day six, she is very fragile emotionally, and doesn't have the energy she has when she starts the series. I suppose that is normal for anyone receiving chemotherapy, but it is very hard to watch. I know there is nothing I can do to help, so I try and not get in the way, but do what I can to take some of the chores away from her. We keep praying for complete healing but only time will tell.

I believe that Gerda is the most courageous person I have ever known. I read somewhere that traumatic events that occur during the first six years of a child's life will stay with them for their entire life. There is no cure and they must learn to deal with the trauma symptoms when and however they manifest themselves. This is definitely true in Gerda's life. She is afraid of everything. In her mind, anything could explode; you could fall from a bicycle; a stick would poke your eye out; at any time, something bad could happen that had the potential to harm you.

Courage is not absence of fear; it is how you deal with your fear. Gerda mastered her fear. She refused to let it rule her life and she did whatever she was required to do. Right up until now. She has faced death from cancer and looked it right in the eye and said no, I will continue to live, and she has. For the past year, in spite of her chemotherapy we have had an almost normal life. She insists that she can do it and she does it. My heart is filled with admiration and love for this woman who looks at her fears and perseveres. Thank you, Gerda, from the bottom of my heart.

****

October 12, 2016: Gerda's ANC had jumped up to 418, so Doctor Kojouri decided not to begin the Neuprogen but to continue with the Vidaza. He scheduled the 14th series to begin on October 17th. He explained that the chemo was beginning to lose ground to the leukemia and it was only a matter of time until it would stop working at all. He recommended that she continue with the treatment but not to look for a cure. It will continue to work until it doesn't, then Gerda must decide how much she wants to fight the disease.

****

November 1, 2016: Started the month of November with a blood transfusion. The first one since February 15th. That was followed by a platelet transfusion on Friday, November 4th. The blood work does not look promising because all of the important readings are down. Gerda's ANC is around 90 which is very low. She is scheduled to start the 15th series of Vidaza on the 14th of November. We will see how things go during that series.

****

November 20, 2016: She is in the middle of the 15th series of Vidaza and has not required another transfusion. Tomorrow she will have lab work done, and we hope no transfusions. She has not been feeling well for the past few days. Very tired and emotionally distraught. She gets upset very easily and cries at the slightest little thing. She doggedly holds on and does her housework. She washes and cooks and won't let me do any of these things. I watch her and it breaks my heart. Here Gerda is suffering and I cannot do a thing to help her. I am so grateful that she is not in pain. I don't think I could deal with that. It is difficult enough just to watch her fade away.

Doctor Kojouri prescribed an antidepressant, Zoloft, to help ease the emotional stress and her anxiety. After about a week we began to notice a difference in her behavior. Much to my relief, she is more relaxed and she no longer gets upset at the little things that had bothered her before.

****

December 15, 2015: Gerda was scheduled to start round 16 of her Vidaza injections. The blood tests indicated that the treatments are no longer working, so further injections were cancelled. In late November, she had needed a blood transfusion and a few days later a platelet transfusion.

158

All indications are that the Leukemia is winning the war, and a different approach may be required. There is another chemotherapy drug, Dacogen, that is used to treat MDS but also has the potential to fight AML. We weighed the side effects against the possible extension of her life and decided to continue to fight and see if Dacogen works. It will take about three months to determine if it is helping. We realize that there is only about a 30 percent chance that it will help, but 30 percent is worth the gamble. Maybe we are grasping at straws, but we can't give up hope at this point.

****

December 18, 2016: We baked Christmas cookies today. For the past 20 years, we have made Christmas cookies together, and Gerda insisted that we do it this year. She mixes the recipe and I cut out the forms and make the spoon drops. We made three types of cookies and some spicy baked walnuts. By late afternoon she was tired, but we both felt very happy with our days' work. We both smiled a lot.

The tree has been up for a couple of weeks, and we are looking forward to Christmas with the family. Gerald, Betsy, Melinda and Sophia will be here on Christmas Eve and Melinda and Sophia will stay the night and Christmas day. Gerda is going to make good German potato salad with hot *Fleischwurst* for Christmas eve and *Sauerbraten* on Christmas day. Both are family favorites. It will be a good time in spite of what else is happening.

****

Lyle E. Herbaugh

January 1, 2017: Christmas came and went but not the way we had planned. Sophia and Melinda both had the flu and were unable to come. With Gerda's immune system being compromised they didn't want to come and expose her to the flu. Gerald called and asked if Betsy's two grown kids could come for Christmas Eve. We love them both and were happy to have them spend the evening with us. It turned out to be a quiet Christmas. Gerda and I were alone Christmas day. She read a book she had gotten from me and I did my annual puzzle.

This was the first time since Sophia was born that she and Melinda were not with us on Christmas. After seventeen years, we had become accustomed to sharing this time with the two of them, and without them it seemed like the house was empty and lonely.

Gerda started a new chemotherapy drug last week and it is infused every day for 10 days. Because the Cancer Care Center is closed over the weekends, Gerda was admitted to the hospital and received her infusions while an inpatient. I spent New Year's Eve alone at home and she was alone in her hospital room. We were both asleep by eleven o'clock.

****

January 7, 2017: We took down the Christmas tree today and put all of the Christmas and Advent decorations away in the garage for another year. We are both aware that this was probably our last Christmas and New Year, so we were very disappointed that it went down the way it did.

Gerda's condition has slowly gone downhill and she requires frequent blood and platelet transfusions. The new chemo may help but it will take about three months before we can expect to see improvements in her blood condition. We continue to hope and pray for healing, but that has not happened yet.

She is starting to show the effects of so many blood draws and IV infusions. There are bruises in several places on both her arms and some on her legs and body. We don't know how long this will go on and when or how it will end. We only know that at some point it will end.

Through the months of her illness we talked a lot about our lives together. In spite of the rough beginning we have had a wonderful life together. There are so many happy memories that I am sometimes overwhelmed with emotion.

I remember the Christmases when the kids were little; the many vacations in Denmark with long walks on the beach and the evenings sitting by the fireplace eating popcorn. The many road trips crisscrossing the country, seeing deer and antelope by the hundreds; meeting so many nice folks everywhere we traveled. The man in Paris Texas who served us cold watermelon and refused to let us pay because I was in the service; the sunsets; the beautiful flowers; the time spent with our grandchildren, and the times we just sat together doing nothing, saying nothing, each content to be with the other. So many memories.

Life has been good to us both and I am so pleased that we were able to spend our lives together. Gerda was an extraordinary partner to me and for all the years, wherever I stood, she stood beside me. Whatever I did, she supported me. She was always there for me. After 57 years, I say thank you from the bottom of my heart, and I love you very much! When the time comes, I will join you soon, and I will see you in heaven.

****

The following sums up her feelings about her life:

I have lived a wonderful life
I loved and
I was loved in return
I brought life into the world
I cared for my children
I cared for my husband
I traveled
I experienced what others
Can only dream of.
There were ups and downs
Some rough spots
And hardships to overcome
But I survived and
Gave thanks for my good fortune.
I lived long and I prospered.

CPSIA information can be obtained
at www.ICGtesting.com
Printed in the USA
FSHW020319120919
61936FS